TO PHILIP
  BURKE.
MARCH 2022.

About the Author

The author was born in Greenwich, south east London on 31st May 1947. At five years of age, he was placed into a loving foster home and at eight years old, was dragged out of that home, kicking and screaming. Life from then on was one of degradation and poverty.

The days of wine and roses
   are now gone Patrick,
the same fate awaits us both,
but 'nil desperandem',
we will search, one day,
the star's above
   as we used to
      here on earth.

Cancer Patient and Other Jottings

Michael T Moran

Cancer Patient and Other Jottings

Olympia Publishers
London

www.olympiapublishers.com
OLYMPIA PAPERBACK EDITION

Copyright © Michael T Moran 2022

The right of Michael T Moran to be identified as author of
this work has been asserted in accordance with sections 77 and 78
of the Copyright, Designs and Patents Act 1988.

All Rights Reserved

No reproduction, copy or transmission of this publication
may be made without written permission.
No paragraph of this publication may be reproduced,
copied or transmitted save with the written permission of the
publisher, or in accordance with the provisions
of the Copyright Act 1956 (as amended).

Any person who commits any unauthorised act in relation to
this publication may be liable to criminal
prosecution and civil claims for damage.

A CIP catalogue record for this title is
available from the British Library.

ISBN: 978-1-80074-094-5

First Published in 2022

Olympia Publishers
Tallis House
2 Tallis Street
London
EC4Y 0AB

Printed in Great Britain

Dedication

IN LOVING MEMORY OF MUMMY LADE AND JANE

CANCER PATIENT ONE
THE BEGINNING

He cleared his throat
and began to speak.
"Mr Moran...
I regret to inform you
that you have contracted cancer."
He sat back in his swivel chair,
did a few little twists in it,
tapped his pen on the rim of a teacup
and then contemplated the ceiling.

He did not seem
to show any regret, indeed
his chubby face was one of cheeriness; he might just as well
have been bestowing a verdict
of 'Cancer Free'.

He withdrew his eyes from the ceiling,
jumped from his seat and said,
"There are various specialists you have to see."
So we went from room to room and in every room
there was gloom and doom...
all my top teeth
had to be extracted

in preparation
for radiology treatment…
"No," I said, "I am not losing my teeth."
These teeth had cost me £5000 thirty years ago
for crowns and a bridge.
"Impossible," cried the crowd,
"Your teeth would rot in your head
with the effects of radiation."
Jesus, it was like being pole axed.

Later on, when all the heads
had stopped jawing,
they took a blood test,
weighed me
and handed me various booklets
and pamphlets.
'Living with Cancer' etcetera.

To be honest,
most of what they said had passed me over,
it was all a blur;
I was in a state of shock.

Eventually, I found myself
outside the hospital,
where my dear son-in-law
was waiting
in the car.
I slumped in the seat.
"It's cancer Keith, let's go home."

Keith just stared at me.
Then he started the car
and we headed homewards.

On the way, I sat staring out
at the London crowds,
enjoying the late afternoon sun. Three youths running
for a bus,
young mothers pushing buggies:
pink faced cherubs within.
A group of drinkers
sat at a table
outside a pub,
one with a Jack Russel on his lap,
feeding beer to the dog.
This is the normal world
but for me,
a dark, grim world
had just begun.

When I arrived home
I gave my three daughters
the verdict.
Naturally, they took it badly.

I sloped off
to my bedroom alone
and tried to come to terms with the day's events.

So here, within me,

was this disease,
eating me alive
and there was nothing
I could do about it.

There was a full moon that night
and seeing the beauty of the night sky,
I wept for
the first and only time.
My thoughts suddenly turned to those of suicide.
With suicide
I could kill the filthy excretia?
that had entered my body.
But the coward in me
shrunk from would-be suicide;
I could not do it and knew
I never would.

Anyway, it may be that
I could be cured after all.
The medics had said that facial cancer
is the most easily cured.
Well, wait and see;
we will wait and see.

Strangely, I slept soundly that first night
and I awoke
with a sense of hope.

My daughters left

at noon and at last,
I was alone
with my own company.

As we said,
"Wait and see,
wait and see…"
To pray?
It's no good now,
praying to God…
He knew only too well
that I never prayed
to Him,
never asked for help
even on those occasions
when I desperately needed it.

I was always the raging atheist and would curse Him
when things went against me, which perversely shows
that I must have had
a curious belief in Him.

See,
I even subconsciously acknowledge
Him when writing of Him
with the saintly capital letters of G and H.

But I refuse to be a hypocrite now, not now that I am
living these,
my darkest hours.

There will be no holy, blinding light when I die.
No angel coming down
to take me to paradise.
Death will be
like the switching off of a lamp and then oblivion,
perfect peace and oblivion;
that is all I want after death.

SWEEPER OF THE STREETS

The street sweeper prays no more
for the luxuries of life, an immense lottery win
to attain a penthouse
overlooking the Thames, a dream car,
a cute dolly for a wife,
a butler, housekeeper, a cook.

All those things he desired,
nay — prayed for,
yearning to acquire the good life.
Now after countless duff lottery tickets,
he at last, realises that he was destined
for a lifetime of poverty.
He even offered Lucifer his soul in return
for all that he coveted but old nick,
of course, was otherwise engaged.

So now
he sweeps the streets,
not thinking of anything in particular,
his eyes are dead
with the overwhelming emptiness that engulfs him.
He sweeps up
the tide of detritus discarded by mankind,

not even bothering
to call the public 'cunts' any more.

He goes home each night,
to his high-rise council flat
on the 10th floor.

The lift is not working:
it has been vandalised again.
Wearily, he climbs the stairs,
splashing through pools of urine
on the stairwells.
Eventually, he opens the door
of the flat
and finds his ugly, fat wife drunk again,
no dinner on the table again.
He curses and flops down
on the worn and holed settee.

Later, he falls asleep
in front of the television.
Later still, he is roused from his stupor
by his wife,
screeching with drunken laughter
at an episode of the 'The Simpsons'.
He pulls himself up from the settee
and leaves the flat to buy a takeaway,
a burger and fries;
with nothing in his head
except the unrelenting misery of his existence.

IN LONDON'S WEST END

The tramp,
in his wheelchair,
begged me for fifty pence
as I walked past him;
I naturally ignored him.
He shouted out to me
and to my surprise,
there was no abuse,
no expletives,
just a few soulful words:
"God bless you anyway".
I turned and walked back to him.
His face was like worn and weather-beaten,
crinkled, black leather.
His home? Three bags tied to the wheelchair with string.
He looked at me anxiously,
with bloodshot eyes
and with a lifetime's defeat in them.
He raised his hands
but was without aggression,
it was a gesture of surrender.
"I am so sorry sir,
I meant no offence…"
his cultured voice trailed off.
He was a genuine gentleman of the road.
I was amazed at his accent:

it smacked of Eton and a twenty-bedroom mansion.
The only thing was the stench
surrounding him: excreta, urine and
Christ knows what else.
I had to get away
and reached for my wallet
to give him a five-pound note,
which he gracefully accepted and said:
"I was not always like this, sir
but I thank you, it is most appreciated."
I told him to get a good meal
and patted his shoulder,
I then walked away.
"God bless," he said as I turned away.
After some seconds
I looked back. His head was resting
on the back of his
battered, old wheelchair
and his eyes were closed.
I wondered what life had dealt him
to end up this way:
a woman? Drugs?
It was quite obvious
that he was not long for this world.
Just then my bus arrived
and I boarded it.
I looked out of the window.
He was still in the same position,
head back, eyes closed
whilst all of London passed him by. There but for fortune…

A DAY IN THE LIFE OF A YOUNG MAN CIRCA 1965

A bright, sunny Friday morning,
he rises from his bed
to greet the new day;
the sunshine, most welcome.

He dresses in his mod gear,
the flowered shirt
with button-down collar,
the hipster jeans,
the leather, Beatle's jacket,
the Cuban-heeled boots
with chiselled toes...

Feeling good,
he saunters downtown to Woolwich,
looking at himself
in the reflective shop windows
and enters the mod's restaurant
where his mod pals
are already situated.
He orders a full fry-up
and talks to his mates,
while waiting for his meal.

The plan was to meet up the next day
at dawn, in Beresford Square
and leave en-masse
for the long trip to Brighton,
in search of rockers
and to punch rocker heads.

After his meal
and much planning with his mates,
he left and went home
to clean and polish his pride and joy:
a blue Lambretta T.V 175cc scooter
with chrome side panel
and all the mod extras.
He had owned many scooters
but the T.V 175
was the fastest of them all;
even outperforming the sporty S.X.200.

Later,
he was lying on his bed,
listening to the latest John Mayall album
on his Bang and Olufsen stereo,
when the doorbell rang.
It was only Linda —
a girl he knew.
They had coffee,
took a couple of 'uppers'
and then had frantic sex

on the floor, with the music of 'The Pretty Things'
playing in the background.
Linda eventually left and he showered.
Oh, how he loved life
in that moment of time!
He was going to live forever!

A DAY IN THE LIFE OF AN OLD MAN CIRCA 2009

It is only when a man has reached his sixties that he realises
the dreams, plans and ambitions of his youth
are now unobtainable, in this,
his near dotage.

So now,
he takes a back seat
when family and friends visit — virtually silent.
He lets his wife
do the chitter chatter. You see,
he is too overwhelmed
with boredom and depression and the continual futility
of his life.

When alone,
he sits staring out of the window at the reflected sunlight
of the bobbing, dappled leaves on the elm tree,
swaying in the breeze outside his window.
For hours he sits like this.

It's 2 a.m.
He reaches for the sleeping pills
and swallows a temazepam,
in order to give him a comforting high
before bedtime.
He places one pill
in his cache
of suicide pills,
which is hidden
and is his passport
to the next world,
if life becomes intolerable.
Later, he climbs the stairs slowly.
His wife is snoring loudly.
He curses and heads for the spare room
and sleepy, oblivion…
Until tomorrow and the nightmare of his life.

THE FIRST TIME I WAS ABANDONED

My mother placed me in a foster home when I was five years old. I learnt later in life that she had been evicted from her council house through failure to pay the rent. Now, I am not going to write about Mother's irresponsible attitude to life; no, that comes later. I am going to tell you of the family that fostered me.

The husband-and-wife team were Mr and Mrs Lade of Blackheath, South London. I well remember that first night when Mother took me to the Lade's home. I was sat in an armchair whilst Mother and Mrs Lade conversed. The time went by and the next thing I knew and which I could not believe, was Mother waving goodbye to me in the doorway. I let out a yell and cried. I went to get up but Mrs Lade gently restrained me and said, "Hush now, Michael and I will give you another piece of cake. Don't cry, my boy."

So, mother left, and left me bereft; I got my second piece of cake, still crying. Mrs Lade put me at my ease and I ceased weeping eventually. I looked around the oak-panelled sitting room. There was a television set, a radio, the television rare in 1952 and very expensive. Various people: one, a girl who looked a little older than me and was smiling. This girl was Janet, the daughter of the Lades. A young man holding a trumpet. This was

Laurie, approximately twenty years old, son of the Lades and there was Jimmy, a sad-looking boy about my age.

Mr Lade smiled benignly and said, "Don't worry Michael, you will soon settle in."

During my three years at the Lades', they only ever used my full Christian name of Michael, none of that 'Mickey' or 'Mick' rubbish. I was told that the boy called Jimmy was a foster child too and that I was to share a bedroom with him.

Later on, after switching on the television for my benefit, Mrs Lade said, "Come now Michael, I will show you where your bedroom is and Jimmy, you too, it's way past your bedtime."

She took hold of my old, battered suitcase and after saying goodnight, we three went up a long flight of stairs.

"Have you brought a toothbrush Michael?" I looked at her blankly. I didn't know what a toothbrush was. So, she rummaged around in my suitcase, then went off and returned with a toothbrush. She took me to the bathroom and showed me how to brush my pearly whites, which were not so white.

I had no pyjamas or underwear so she got a pair of Jimmy's underpants and a vest. Next thing, I was being tucked up in a crisp, clean, single bed with Jimmy in his bed at the far side of the room.

The light was switched off and we, Jimmy and I, were left in silence in the pitch-black room. I whispered to Jimmy who never, ever said much, then or in the future, "Is it all right here?"

Jimmy shifted in his bed. "They're nice," he said and

that was all. I lay awake for a while, thinking how strange all this was but I felt at ease and fell asleep wondering what tomorrow would bring.

I have been told by various friends and a prison psychiatrist that I have a photographic memory.
If you wonder at my memory when I was five, let me tell you that I can remember things from when I was two years old, like the toy gun that fired ping-pong balls which I received one Christmas and proceeded to shoot the balls at the family cat.

I was woken from my sleep by Mrs Lade, who was the epitome of gentle kindness. It was early in the morning and I soon became used to it for Mrs Lade was not one for lying in bed at all hours of the day.

We went down the stairs, all three of us and I could smell the appetising odour of food being cooked. Jimmy and I were seated side by side, with Janet on the other side of me. Firstly, we had Scott's porridge oats, followed by bacon, eggs, fried bread and fried tomatoes.

I'll never forget that first meal; it was the most delicious food I had ever tasted with the bacon fried to a crisp. It was the first time I'd had this food and it was like manna from the gods, of whom we all had said a prayer to bless the food.

When we had finished breakfast, Mrs Lade took my hand and led me to the bathroom and told me to brush my teeth, day and night. She then bathed me and said that she was going out to do some shopping for me.

When finished, we went down the stairs where she switched on the television for Jimmy and I. Janet prepared for school.

Mrs Lade went off with her daughter. Me and Jimmy were left to ourselves and I was fascinated by the television. It seemed like a magical toy.

Eventually, Mrs Lade returned laden down with shopping bags. She showed me the contents, they were all clothes for me, a pair of sandals and slippers and two sets of pyjamas. She dressed me in a crisp, white shirt and corduroy shorts and placed the slippers on my feet, telling me to never wear shoes in the house, only slippers. Then she said she could do with a cup of tea and would us boys like one? I was really beginning
to like it here and felt totally at ease.

Time went on. Jimmy and I were enrolled at the local primary school, Branfill Junior school. There were some strange kids there. One boy's forte was digging out bogies from his nose and then eating them. Strange: us kids would howl with disgust and wonderment when he placed said bogey on his tongue.

Mrs Lade would take us to school and in the afternoon, pick us up. She was never late, always there, waiting, no wonder I began to call her 'Mummy' which she would correct to 'Mummy Lade'. "Michael, I am not your mother, just add 'Lade' my dear."

Let me tell you dear reader, that I loved Mrs Lade dearly. Always cool, calm and collected and all the time educating me and she taught me to read in no time.

She instilled a Christian outlook on life without trying to brainwash me. As a family, we would all go to church on Sundays and I enjoyed it immensely down to the musty church odour of St. George's, which was just around the corner from 'our' house in Mycenae Avenue.

The circus was in town, camped out on Blackheath Common. Mrs Lade put us three kids in a huddle and said, "Now children, what would you rather have, a visit to the circus or would you rather have a scooter each? Put it to the vote please."

Us kids looked at each other, Janet giggling said, "A scooter, Mummy, please…"

Jimmy said, "I want to go to the circus…"

So, the casting vote was mine. "I'd love a scooter Mummy Lade…"

"Well, that's decided: a scooter each then…"

Poor Jimmy looked disappointed and went upstairs to the bedroom.

After a week or so, the scooters were delivered.

What a frenzy. We ripped off the cardboard packaging to reveal the scooters in all their glory.

Janet picked a pink example whilst I grabbed a red one with whitewall tyres, Jimmy was left with the remaining black example.

What times Janet and I had, racing each other down the road. We had such good laughs. Poor Jimmy was always crashing his scooter or worse, falling from it.

Television in those days was shut down for most of the day, with a 'test card' being the only picture that was displayed. Around 5 p.m., the programs would start — children's films such as 'The Cisco Kid', 'Bill and Ben the flowerpot men' etc. We would sit transfixed at the flickering black and white screen.

My birth mother would come to see me now and then. Some two years had elapsed and she began to observe me with sadness in her eyes. I was more pre-occupied with my life with the Lades. I had been hijacked with love from the family. My natural mother was fast becoming a stranger to me. As a child, I did not think anything of my mother's feelings as she observed me slipping away from her. I now know what I did not at that time, that my idyllic life with the Lades was destined to end…

One summer, in the splendid garden of the Lades and on a scorching hot day, Mr Lade tied a hosepipe to the trellis with the metal nozzle pointing down. Jimmy and I were stripped down to our underpants and Janet donned a swimsuit. Amidst much hilarity, we ran beneath the nozzle of the hose pipe gushing out ice cold water. Jimmy, poor Jimmy, he ran under the nozzle of the hose and took a tremendous leap at it and cracked his head open.

What a great to-do there was with blood gushing everywhere. "First-aid box," Mrs Lade shouted and Mr Lade went to get it. Between them, they patched up the sobbing Jimmy with antiseptic cream and a bandage around his head, which looked like a turban.

Needless to say, the hosepipe was quickly dismantled and put away. Yes, I'm afraid our Jimmy was accident-prone: he was always in scrapes of some kind.

One day, sometime after my arrival at the Lade's, Mrs Lade awoke Jimmy and me and said to us that we were all going to London to see our new Queen, Elizabeth the second. The whole family were going, with Mr Lade to drive us there in his brand, new motor car.

After we had eaten, we went to his garage and clambered aboard the Vauxhall with us kids waving our Union Jacks. We made our way to central London where Mr Lade found somewhere to park. We then walked to where the Royal procession was to pass. There were thousands of people all armed with Union Jacks.

Somehow, we all managed to get a good vantage point with all the children at the front. Then came a mighty roar in the distance, our new Queen was on her way. I leaned further out to get the best view but a smiling copper gently pushed me back; my first brush with the law.

The Queen's carriage was now in sight and the roaring of the crowd was tremendous. The carriage was now level with us and I frantically waved my little Union Jack but her majesty chose that moment to turn her face to the crowds on the opposite side of the road and in a flash, the carriage went on its way.

Every detail of that day is etched in my memory. Queen Elizabeth the second has been with me for most of my life, a most benign and gracious monarch; long may she reign.

The years passed at the Lades'; three happy years. I was joyously happy, content and loved. The family were thoroughly devoid of any injustice, nastiness or immorality. 'Give me a boy at seven and I will give you the man', so the quote goes. But my beautiful life with these wonderful people was about to end.

One afternoon, after school, Mrs Lade took me aside and we went to the peace of the front room. I could see she had been crying by her red eyes. She sat me down and spoke softly to me. Gazing at me, she said my mother was going to take me away that night. I could not grasp it. I said, "Why Mummy, don't you want me any more?"

She hugged me, her voice was choked, she said that she loved me dearly, that she had to obey my mother's wishes.

"Mummy, I don't want to go…" "Please don't let her take me." I could not grasp the enormity of all this and burst into tears which rolled down my face. Hot tears, burning… I felt I was going to die. Mrs Lade and I hugged, clinging onto each other, both crying…

My foster mummy, Mrs Lade, took me up to the bedroom and started to pack my belongings. I looked out of the old window for the last time. It was a rainy winter's night, dark and bleak. I began to weep again.

Mrs Lade said, "Hush now Michael, you can always come back and see us." At that moment in time, I hated my birth mother.

Later, we sat in the dining room awaiting the arrival of 'Mother'. Janet was crying and Jimmy looked downcast. Mummy Lade made us all a cup of tea and after that, we sat quietly and waited.

Before long, we heard a hubbub of noise and the

doorbell rang. My stomach churned and I thought I was about to be sick. Mrs Lade took my hand and we all went to the front door.

She opened it to show a large group of people: my birth mother included and also my father who I had not seen for three years. I looked at them all and a surge of anger took hold of me. That furious anger that I felt many times in my forthcoming life.

I threw the suitcase at my mother and kicked my father on the shin. "Little bastard," he yelled, rubbing his shinbone.

"WE WILL HAVE NONE OF THAT LANGUAGE HERE," Mrs Lade shouted.

That was the one and only time I heard her speak in anger. I then raced back into the house; I was not giving up without a fight and hid behind a sofa.

A whole body of people, some of whom I did not know, came up the passage and grabbed me. My father grabbed my arms and Ken Vince (a future brother-in-law) had hold of my legs. I struggled and kicked and bawled my eyes out but of course, it was futile.

They carried me out into the street and the front door was closed. My idyllic life with the Lade family had also closed. I never saw them again.

They took me down the road passed St. George's church where I had spent many a happy hour. Eventually, we stopped at a bus stop. The menfolk put me down and gave me dire warnings as to what would happen if I ran off. They needn't have worried for I had already resigned myself to fate but I cried; Lord how I cried.

My mother knelt down and spoke softly to me. She said that I was going to stay with one of my sisters who lived in Essex and that this sister had three boys of her own and that I would like it there. I did not say anything to her, I was still sobbing.

The mental anguish and pain of that dreadful night scarred me for life. It is as real to me as if it happened yesterday. In later years, I would ask my mother why she took me away from the Lades. She would become angry at these questions and refused to speak. But I guess I knew the answer. Whilst at the Lades', I had slipped away from her and had made the Lade family, objects of my love. I was growing up in a middle-class environment so totally at odds with the life of my mother. To put it simply, Mother was jealous.

The group of us took various modes of public transport and after what seemed an age, we arrived at my sister's house in Aveley, Essex. We trooped into the living room where a man was sitting in an armchair with a boy on his lap. This man was Colin Wood, husband of my half-sister. I sat on a chair and glanced over at the man. He looked at me with contempt (I was still crying) and then looked away, as if he had looked at a steaming turd.

That was all I needed. I shouted to my mother, "I am not staying here… I want to go back to Mrs Lade."

She said, "What on earth is the matter, Mickey?"

I said, "That man hates me."

'That man' turned out to be my sister's husband, Colin. He feigned surprise at my outburst and stammered indignantly denying any such thing.

My inept mother said, "Don't worry Colin, he is just upset."

So, there you are, ten minutes in the house and I had already made enemies as my sister was looking daggers at me. I was in total despair; how was I to live with such people? That thought plunged me into a spiral of anxiety.

Eventually, I found myself in a freezing cold bed in a freezing cold room shared with the three Wood boys. I lay awake for hours. My initial feelings about Mr and Mrs Wood were to prove correct but I had no idea just how horrific my life was going to be under the 'care' of these two sadists.

After the peace and sanity of the Lade household, my introduction to life with my half-sister was a staggering mental shock, which affected me for the rest of my life.

When I awoke on that first morning in Aveley, I looked out of the window to a scene of snow and grey skies, total depression. I still could not grasp the calamitous events of the day before.

Pondering over it gave me a severe headache. I had been taken from the love and security of my foster home to unfriendly, hostile people who, it seemed, were deeply resentful of my presence and so it proved to be, with hardly anyone speaking to me, no secure environment, no love, no love, NO LOV E.

In the forthcoming pages, you will read of the unrelenting hate and malice I suffered at the hands of my sister. The treatment meted out to me was callous, cruel, vicious and inhuman.

In later life, I realised that my sister suffered serious mental disorders. She hated me and despite her parlous mental state, I ended up loathing her for the rest of my life.

THE WAY OF THE WORLD

The brand, new Mercedes
smacked into the rear of Vic's old banger.
We all got out
to survey the damage,
'twas a small dent in the nearside bumper.
The driver of the Mercedes
got out of his car and said,
with a cultured, gasping voice,
"I am frightfully sorry chap's,
I will pay for the damage of course."
Vic's eyes lit up.
The Merc driver
stank of alcohol. Vic knew
he was about to have a right good result.
Vic said, "£200 mate but
I want the cash now."
The Merc said,
"But it's only a little dent. £200? Really?"
"Well, we will get the cops and
go through the insurance then," said Vic.
The Merc got out his bulging wallet
and, tight-lipped, counted out the money,
went back to his car and drove
off down the street like a lunatic.

We all laughed and turned to Vic.
"You lucky bastard," I said to him.
If the other driver had only known
that at the end of the week,
Vic was going to scrap the old banger
when his new car arrived
from the showroom.

The gang of us had a great time
up the west-end that night,
all due to a drunk driver
and Vic's greedy bite.

THE GOOD, THE BAD AND THE UGLY
TEVIOT AVENUE, AVELY, ESSEX 1955

I had four sisters or to be precise, four half-sisters. All four were much older than me, their father died when they were very young and, years later, my mother married again and out popped yours truly.

Two of the sisters were good to me and on occasions, my mother would palm me off to live with them, one or t'other. They had small children of their own but they always found room for me, two sisters who treated me kindly with love and care.

Sister number one gave me a birthday present one year, of a 'Hopalong Cassidy' boy's wristwatch, with a picture of Hopalong Cassidy on the dial, circa 1955. I cherished it for a long time and continued wearing it long after it ceased to function.

Sister number two was just as kind to me as sister number One.

She would 'feed me up' saying, "Come on Mickey, eat it all, we have got to get some meat on those bones."

On Sunday nights she would let me stay up late to listen to the radio and the weekly serial entitled 'Journey Into Space': an excellent BBC Drama aimed at an audience who had space travel fever.

I loved my time with sister number two, mainly

because she allowed me to stay off school if I wanted to. "You don't want to go? You don't have to go," she would say with a grin.

Many years later she contracted lung cancer for she had, a sixty cigarettes a day, habit. I went to see her in hospital the day before she died. She was very weak and could barely raise her arms but she could still crack a joke and gave me that same old grin, as we talked about the old days.

Much later, I took my leave of her and kissed her gently on the cheek. I took a last look at her through the window of the door, her head on the pillow, gazing out at the cloudless, blue sky. I turned and walked quickly away, my deep sorrow got the better of me and I cried.

Sister number three was psychotic. I was placed with her at the age of eight years and Christ, she made my life a living hell. Always, she would scream abuse at me for some minor misdemeanour. She never used physical violence but the mental abuse directed at me was just as demoralising. That gut-wrenching, shrill screaming is still with me to this day producing cold shudders down my spine whenever I think of her.

If anything ever went wrong in their house, then I got the blame for it. Number three had three sons of her own who were up to all manner of mischief. I was also my sister's servant. She sent me on endless errands to the local shop, a mile away. "Run all the way there and all the way back," she would demand, thrusting her mad face into mine.

Once, I came back from the shop and was a penny

short in the change, she screamed and hollered so much that it scared the shit out of me. She then made me stand in a corner facing the wall. I was to stand there until her dim-witted husband came home from work; that fuckrie. When informed of the missing penny, he thrust his face into mine, shook his head and said, "What are we going to do with you?" and tut-tutted incessantly.

I would rack my brains wondering why she hated me. I couldn't understand it. I never had any problems but I was always in trouble in that house, which stood on a bleak and desolate council housing estate in semi-rural Essex.

She was tight with food — often I would go to bed with a ravenous hunger. Once, when she had me buttering bread in preparation for tea, I stuffed a slice of bread in my mouth. I was driven to it by sheer hunger. As luck would have it, she returned to the kitchen just as I was beginning to choke on the bread. Jesus. There was hell to pay and all the while the bread was dropping out of my mouth, while sister number three ranted and raved and said that I was not going to have any food at tea-time as my punishment.

Number three would have me peeling potatoes, shelling peas, doing the washing-up and drying-up, sweeping the floors, mopping the floors and always there were runs to the dreaded shop a mile away.

At night, I would gaze out of the bedroom window and beg God to help me, which he never did. When I realised that I was not going to receive any holy help I stopped praying and, in all my life through, I never asked Him again.

My feckless mother would come every Saturday to give me a few bob pocket money, and pay the witch money for my keep. One Saturday came total salvation. My mother had arrived and was in conversation with number three in the kitchen. Suddenly, I heard the screaming voice that I knew only too well. "I'm not going to keep your Irish brat for thirty shillings a week."

Alarmed, I ran into the kitchen and saw my mother, who appeared very sad and was not speaking. She came over to me, put her arm around me and took me to my bedroom. "I'm taking you out of here, Mickey," she said, as she pulled out my old suitcase from under the bed. I could not believe it, was I about to escape the clutches of the witch? As I watched my mother packing my bits, I realised that it was, at last, over and that I was bound for a new life, away from the screaming harridan, away from the drudgery of all those household chores, away from those dreaded runs to the shop. My mother said that sister number three had wanted more money for my keep; money which she did not have. She shouted at my mother, "I'm not keeping your Irish brat on thirty shillings a week!" Mother and I left the house, and although I was elated, I noticed that Mum was crying so I put my arm around her waist and said, "Don't worry Mum, we will be okay."

On the walk to the green-line bus stop I kept looking back, fearful that the witch was following, wielding a kitchen knife. I only felt safe once we were on the bus which was roaring towards London Town and freedom at last.

We arrived at Fulham in south west London and took a final bus to the area where my mother lived. She had the basement 'flat', one room with a tiny adjoining kitchen. I was still in a hysteria of elation and said to Mum that I could easily live here.

She ruffled my hair and with a sad smile said, "Don't worry any more, we will not see her again. I'm sorry boy." She started to cry and then came a bombshell. She said we were to leave first thing in the morning and that she owed the landlord three weeks' rent. She hadn't seen my father for three weeks and had just twenty-five shillings, enough to get us to her Aunt Gert's in Pembury, Kent. We were to leave early the next day in what is commonly known as a 'moonlit flit'.

I was full of questions and alarm; I could not believe that it was going to start over again. She reassured me that all would be well. It was her Aunt Gert that we were going to live with and that I would enjoy life there.

We settled down eventually and she made a mound of spam sandwiches of which I devoured the lot, for I had a fearful hunger. We listened to the radio for a while, then she said we should sleep as we had an early start. I was quite excited at the prospect of the 'moonlit flit' and looked forward to the morning.

I slept on cushions placed on the floor and slept soundly with a full stomach, which was a strange experience after the perpetual hunger in the witch's house.

I was almost nine years of age and intermittently, over the forthcoming years, I would awake in a sweat at night after a nightmare which featured sister number three attacking me with a carpet beater, or at other times, a huge wooden stick. These dreams went on for a number of years and only ceased when I reached adolescence.

Number three infected my consciousness deeply. Even now at the age of seventy-two, the mere thought of her fills me with foreboding. She emigrated to Australia with her family, around 1965. Relations and friends, a large gang of them, saw them off at a railway station in Central London. I did not attend. I never saw her again. She died in 1999.

It's a fact that I readily admit to the reader, that I had the world's worst parents; unbelievably feckless and irresponsible. But despite this, I loved them dearly. They were like children and I was Father to them.

We rose at 6 a.m. and prepared to leave. After Mother finished packing, she sat me down and with a serious face, she spoke to me. She said that this time she really was going to leave my father. Seeing the doubtful look on my face, she reassured me quickly, emphatically stating that she meant it this time; IT WAS OVER. She went on to say that she had contacted her Aunt Gert with a view to living with her for a while and the aunt had readily agreed. Mother had been given her aunt's name 'Gert', a name she disliked — calling herself 'Ann' to all and sundry.

A little later, we tip-toed up the stairs, my mother shushing me all the way up. On the ground floor, she left the door keys and a note in an envelope, propped up against the landlord's door. A few steps down the passage, out the front door and we were gone, like thieves in the night.

GREAT-AUNT GERT

We took various buses and trains and eventually found our way to Pembury. Mother, hard-up as she was, took a taxi, the fare almost cleaned her out and at long last, we were standing on Aunt Gert's doorstep. There was a large, polished, brass knocker in the form of a roaring lion on the huge front door. Mother rapped twice. I swear the sound was so loud that I could hear it echoing within the house.

The door was opened by a little, old, wizened lady with a cigarette hanging from her lips. Great Aunt Gert and Mother embraced and Aunt Gert said, "Come in me dears, come in, you must be tired. Come and I will make you a pot of tea."

She led us down a long hallway and into the kitchen where there was the wonderful aroma of baking bread. The food prospects seemed to be good. The kitchen was neat, clean and tidy with antique furniture and china nick-nacks dotted here and there. I liked it here already.

I found my great Aunt staring at me. "Why boy, you are skin and bone, whatever have you been doing to yourself?"

"I'll tell you later Aunt," said my mother, with a guilty glance at me.

"A slice of bread and home-made plum jam, that will

do you until dinner time." It's steak and kidney pie tonight." She winked and smiled at me.

Doubts I had vanished and my heart lifted. "Thank you, Great Aunt," I said emphatically. My happiness was total. I had landed on my feet. Such was the warm and cosseting comfort that I had not felt for a long, long time.

That night, after a most delicious dinner, I was nodding off in an armchair in the warm kitchen, when Aunt Gert said, "Come on boy, let's get you tucked up."

She took me up to a large bedroom which had many antique clocks all ticking and chiming. She placed a mug of cocoa on the bedside table, kissed me on the cheek and said goodnight. With a full stomach that night, I slept like the proverbial log.

I awoke the next morning to the sound of half a dozen clocks chiming. I walked around the bedroom peering at each clock. Some were very beautiful indeed. There were marble, bronze and wooden cases. They had a magical effect on me. I was wholly intrigued by them.

I dressed and descended the many stairs and made my way into the kitchen, lured by the appetising smell of frying bacon. "Hallo me lovely, did you sleep well?"

"I did, thank you Great Aunt," I replied.

"Sit yourself down and I will make you a breakfast."

My mother was sat at the table eating hers. She smiled at me and patted my head. I felt wonderful, total normality reigned but I felt a cold shiver down my spine, when I compared the present, to the misery I had experienced at the home of sister number three.

Aunt Gert had a lodger, an elderly man named Alec,

who spent his days in a large shed at the bottom of the garden. He used to take all his meals in there. Aunt Gert was a common sight, going up the garden path clutching a tray.

There was a faded, red armchair in the shed and on many occasions, I would take a peek through the window to see Alec fast asleep in the old armchair, his smoking pipe clenched between blackened teeth.

Sometimes he would hail me and send me to the local shop which was very near. "Get me a tiffin ol' bor and get one for yourself."

A 'tiffin' was a delicious chocolate bar full of hazelnuts: price sixpence (two and a half pence).

He was a good man, an innocent, old countryman. He had gone, unscathed, through five years in the trenches of the first world war. I would plead with him to see his medals but he would become sullen. "You don 't wanna see them ol' bor."

Aunt Gert sent me a letter when I was sixteen years old. She said that Alec was dead. He had gone up to the main road and had thrown himself under the wheels of an articulated lorry. The man had died instantly. He was seventy-five years old. I became depressed for weeks on receiving that news and pondered long and hard as to WHY DID HE DO IT? Was it perhaps because of his war experiences? I hope he rests in peace for all eternity, for he was a shining beacon of light and good in this dark, grim world.

The weeks flew by at Pembury. This old rambling house with its many rooms was magic to a nine-year-old kid. Every room was filled to bursting, with clocks and beautiful antique furniture. The clocks all worked, loud ticking and chiming prevailed throughout the house and on occasions, the old lady would let me wind the clocks. Aunt Gert was delighted at my interest in them. She would give me little tips about them. "Never fully wind them." "Never turn the hands anti-clockwise." She would often say, "Clocks are living beings, you must care for them."

This love I had for antique clocks stayed with me in later life. I have at least twenty in my living room at present, all loudly ticking and some chiming merrily, just like Aunt's clocks.

My weakness for a timepiece is well-known amongst my fellow antique dealers. Sometimes I have to endure jocular ribbing from them but I don't take offence. They by and large, are the salt of the earth. When I have quiet, retrospective moments with my antiques, polishing and repairing, my thoughts swerve to that remarkable old lady, who set me on to the wonderful world of antique dealing.

Unfortunately for me, my mother enrolled me at the local primary school. On my first day, the teacher stood me up before the entire class and said, "We have a new boy in class today, please make him welcome."

Christ, all those eyes boring into me. I would cringe with embarrassment.

The weeks turned into months. I had bloomed with good health, putting on weight thanks to Great Aunt and the wonderful meals she cooked. She was a lovely, old lady who smoked 'Craven A' cigarettes, always had a fag in her lips, her hair yellow with the stain above her brow which was surrounded by the wispy white of her hair.

She was of saintly temperament, never shouted or lost her temper. At night, she would regale us with tales of her youth when she was 'in service' to the upper classes; the tragic tales of her youth, how she was badly used, the comical tales. I could picture the elite of high Victorian England and was fascinated as I mentally pictured the shenanigans of our 'betters'.

Aunt Gert never married. Her beautiful, old house filled with magnificent antiques, was bought with the generous legacy left to her by no less a person than a Duchess.

It was on just such a night that my old man came calling. Bang, bang, bang. The crashing of the huge knocker on the front door made me jump out of my skin, it almost shook the house. My heart almost stopped when I heard the very faint singing of my old man.

No, please God, don't let it be him. But it was, of course.

Mother and Aunt Gert looked at each other and did not move. Mum then jumped from her seat and rushed down the long hall and as she passed me, I saw her face all lit up and full of anticipation. I could have cried. In that single moment, I realised that the idyllic life here in Kent, for me, was going to end.

Mother let him in and led him down the long hall. He staggered drunkenly against the walls, through to the kitchen. My Great-Aunt watched all this with an amused smile. He was plonked into an armchair and he carried on singing. Mum apologised to Aunt-Gert who said, "You had better get him to bed, Gertie."

Devasted, I too went to bed. I loved my father but when he was around, it could only end in trouble and upheaval. I could not get to sleep through worry and anxiety. Eventually, I dropped off, dreaming of my da' singing 'Danny Boy'.

I arose early the next day whilst the rest of the household were still slumbering. I cooked myself some bacon and egg and then sat quietly, contemplating the future and the hell it might bring. It all hinged on what my old man had planned. The anxiety was overwhelming; my guts were performing somersaults.

I took a walk in the garden. It was a dull, grey morning that matched my mood. The threatening clouds seemed a prophesy of things to come. It began to spit with rain so I returned to the house to find Great-Aunt Gert and Alec in the kitchen with Aunt cooking Alec's breakfast.

Alec, despite the rain, took his tray and wandered off to his beloved shed in the garden. Aunt Gert and I were alone so I took the opportunity to talk to her. I told her that my parents were probably going to take me away and tearfully begged her to let me stay with her and Alec.

She was serious and concerned
and replied, "Michael, you could stay here for as long as you wished but it depends on your mother's wishes: what she wants for you. That is all I can say my dear."

I thanked her profusely, she was a wonderful lady. I had some hope. All I had to do was persuade my mother.

My parents came down shortly afterwards. Mellintrop, in a jovial mood, pseudo-flirted with Great-Aunt to which she laughed and slapped his hand saying, "Gertie, control your husband."

Mellintrop was a great charmer but only when he was sober, which he rarely was.

After they had their meal, my Da' went out into the garden to hunt out old Alec. I wondered what Alec would make of him. I asked Mother how he, my Da', had found us. The reply was that my vindictive sister, the Aveley beast, gave him our address. Mother wrote to her asking for some items of my clothing that had been left behind during our hasty departure from Aveley. Mum never received the clothing. All that arrived was the loved but dreaded, Mellintrop.

"Why did you give our address away, why?"

She remained silent.

She was as venomous as a bucket full of rattlesnakes, was sister number three.

I had to learn of my future. "What's going to happen to me, Mum?"

She was silent and cast down her eyes. Then she spoke, her voice trembling. "Your father has found us somewhere to live, in Fulham, but the landlord's rule is no children." She reverted back to silence.

"What's going to happen to me then?" I asked once again, this time with sheer anger.

She squirmed in her seat looking very guilty and

would not look me in the eye. At last, she said that I was to live with my father's sister, my Aunt Kitty and her husband, Uncle Paddy, all just arrived from Ireland, with their children. They had bought a house in Fulham and apparently, I would be 'most welcome'.

Jesus, not again, I thought to myself. How much more of this life was I to endure? I cried and pleaded with her to let me stay here at Aunt Gert's.

She just shook her head and said she wanted me to live near her in Fulham. That is all she would say. She rose from her seat and disappeared upstairs.

So that was that; I could do no more. All was lost. I mentally cursed my weak mother as I realised that this was all I could expect from her. The only escape was years in the future when I reached adulthood.

Mellintrop was coming down the garden path having conversed with Alec so, not wanting him to catch me crying and with a heavy heart, I traipsed upstairs to my bedroom.

Much later, the bedroom door opened. It was my old man. He walked slowly into the room, sizing me up. "Mickey, you will like your Aunty Kitty, bejesus boy, she wouldn't harm a fly. You'll have a great craic there, boyo."

I looked away without answering. At that, he gave up and just said that we would leave for London tomorrow. With that, he left the room.

So, there it was, no escape for me, all planned and arranged. I didn't have a say in the matter. I cursed God and Mellintrop and punched the fuck out of my innocent pillow. Later, I laid on the bed and fell asleep to the grip of nightmares.

Came the dawn on that dreaded next day, I trooped downstairs in total misery and apprehension in dread of being 'farmed' out yet again to strangers. I made myself a cup of tea and helped myself to one of Aunt Gert's cigarettes which made me choke. I sat, waiting for the household to arise. Eventually, they came down, one by one.

After they had all breakfasted, my old man got up and slapped his hands together. "Come now, let's get ready, we have a long day ahead. Micky, have you packed your case, boyo?"

I did not answer. I had packed but fuck him. I wasn't going to acknowledge his jovial mood.

Later, when all was made ready, we grouped together by the front door apart from old Alec. I put down my suitcase and went into the garden up to Alec's shed.
I peered through the window and there he was of course, puffing on his pipe. I went in, the clouds of smoke swirled out through the open door. "I have to say goodbye, Alec," I said.

He grunted and rummaged in his waistcoat pocket and gave me a two-shilling piece (ten pence). He said, "It's a shame bor, you look artur yoursen, because no other bugger will," and gave me a knowing wink. I left him sitting in his old armchair and went back to the gathering in the hall.

There were tears aplenty including mine. My very dear Great-Aunt put her poor withered arms around me and then shoved a one-pound note in my jacket pocket. I protested but she said, "Buy a new Hopalong Cassidy watch, one that works," she said through her tears.

We went to the coach stop and caught a green-line bus into town, then we boarded a train, then another train that would take us to London. Despite their cajoling, I refused to talk, preoccupied with worry as to my future.

We finally pulled into London Bridge Station and the smoke of old London Town. It goes without saying that Mellintrop and Mother found the nearest pub. They had me stand outside, a glass of lemonade in my hand. I was used to this, having spent many an hour standing outside pubs while they boozed it up inside. They became very merry. I peeped around the door. The entire pub was having a singsong.

My thoughts strayed back to Great-Aunt Gert and Alec. It would be dinner time there and I yearned to be with them in the safe, warm and comforting environment of peace and sanity.

At long last, he and she exited the pub. He hailed a taxi and we set off for Michael Road in Fulham S.W.: Aunt Kitty's home.

We arrived and were made welcome. A gaggle of children were dotted all around the living room and I found myself of great interest to them. Uncle Paddy had the deepest, loudest voice I had ever heard. He was tall and well-built. Apparently, he was a builder with his own gang of Irish labourers. Aunt Kitty, in complete contrast, was demure and softly spoken and said very little. She had jet black hair, the hair of her Celtic ancestors. I knew by instinct that there was no harm in them and I mentally thanked the Gods for that.

My ma and da made ready to leave. Da slipped me a ten-shilling banknote. My mother went to kiss me but I turned away from her. She was crying. I had a sudden, sharp, pang of remorse, so I put my arms around her and she hugged me in return, then they left.

After they left, the Drummy kids gathered round me with questions galore, 'what's your name' etc. Uncle Paddy rescued me from the throng with their charming, childish Irish accents. "Come on now, it's bedtime, off you all go," he shouted playfully, in his stentorian voice. The kids ignored him. "Byjasus, get up those stairs or I'll give you such a BELT," he bellowed.

The children, giggling, all made off en masse. I was to learn that Paddy's bark was worse than his bite. In the time I was there, he never once raised his hand to the kids.

Aunt Kitty turned to me and asked if I would like a sandwich and a cup of tea; not half. I was ravenous. A little later, she brought the refreshments which I rapidly devoured whilst Uncle Paddy asked me a few questions.

After I had finished the sandwich and tea, Aunt Kitty led me up to the bedroom which I was to share with Chris and Pat, two of her sons. She left and the two boys and I had a talk. They were okay kids and I remember thinking that life here with the Drummy clan could be quite pleasant. I thanked the gods for that and drifted off to sleep, dreaming of Great Aunt Gert and her clocks.

Life went by at the Drummys' and was quite pleasant. I

soon made pals, boys who lived in the street: Bernie, Keithy and Oojee (David). Life was completely free; you could do exactly as you pleased. My mates and I would travel all over London, bus fares were a pittance. Literally, we travelled everywhere. It mattered not if you arrived home missing dinnertime, no shouting, no dreaded chores.

I enjoyed life here in Fulham apart from schooldays. I went to Harwood Primary school in time for the dreaded test of the Eleven Plus, which I failed.

It was here that I had my first serious fight.

MY FIRST SERIOUS FIGHT

The Battersea funfair was permanently situated in Battersea Park in the 1950s and was a great lure for the kids of London. Me and the rest of the Michael Road mob would save any money that came our way and splurge it in one afternoon's hit at the fair.

Putney Heath suddenly became another attraction when a rumour persisted, that workmen digging a trench on the heath, had found a hoard of gold coins. This rumour spread like wildfire and in all our naive innocence, a gang of us decided to go to the heath to search the grass and we took a bus at a cost of two old pence (about one new pence).

We arrived and split up into pairs, then we proceeded to search the grass for the odd gold coin that may have been dropped. Ah, the optimism of youth.

After scouring the grass for about an hour, we tired of the venture, realising that the golden treasures of Putney Heath were just wishful thinking. One of our group, Bernie McArthy, did manage to find precious metal, a two-shilling silver florin, which was lying on the grass and had obviously dropped out of someone's pocket, when sunbathing perhaps.

We all made off for the nearest sweet shop and bought confectionary and a bottle of Tizer to wash the sweeties down. So, the afternoon wasn't a total loss.

I had not been long in primary school when trouble found me. One dinner time, I had just exited the toilets having enjoyed a threepenny single cigarette supplied by an obliging tobacconist, when I was approached by three tough-looking herberts. They encircled me and one of them snarled in my ear, "I am Kenny Parsons and I am the hard nut here, now, give me your money or I will fucking do yer."

    I grinned, pushed him out of the way and told him to fuck off. I was grabbed from behind and was wrestled to the ground in a head lock. Try as I may, I could not get out of it. He was a strong bastard was our Kenny, so I gave up and said I would give him money and he released me. Once I was on my feet, I grinned at him
and said, "You just made a mistake in letting me go." I lashed a straight left into his stomach and as he doubled up. I smashed him with a right hook aiming for his nose but instead, my fist landed on his eyebrow. He went down, stretched out on the tarmac like a sack of shit. Oh, thank you, my Uncle Jamesy, for all those fighting lessons. I made a threatening move towards his two henchmen who quickly ran off.

    I bent over Kenny and said, "I'm the hard man now you cunt, get up and if you report me, I'll give you a good kicking." I dragged him up by the lapels of his jacket and was very pleased to see a big, purple patch around his eye.

    "Sorry mate. Sorry," he gasped. He limped off,

doubled up and I kicked him up the arse.

"Don't you want my money?" I said, whilst laughing at the so-called hard man.

I was truly the hard man of the school. I protected all the weak, soft and placid kids from the bullies. They would run up to me hotly pursued by some barbarian and hunter became the hunted, as I chased after the bully.

"That's from Mellintrop," I would yell, after I had dished out retribution.

I had the reputation of a lunatic but, whilst I was at that school, bullying ceased. I was a big fish in a little pond. It was a different story when I progressed to secondary school where I was a little fish in a big pond, teeming with hard nuts.

LONDON SPIRIT

Yes, we children had a high old time of it. We travelled all over London, my favourite haunt being the foreshore of 'old Father Thames'. I enjoyed life and the freedom that came with it.

I fast became 'streetwise' and got up to all sorts of tricks and thieving. Shoplifting was my speciality. I once stole five Parker fountain pens from poor old Woolworth's and had to fast leg-it down the street because I had been spotted. I sold the pens during lunch time at school for two shillings each. The kids formed a queue and were highly pleased, so I went back to class, with ten bob in my pocket and well-pleased was I. No wonder Woolies went bust, poor buggers.

The memory of sister number three was now pushed to the back of my mind but I still had awful dreams at night of that desperately ill woman.

The relatively minor crime of shoplifting gave way to my indulgence in more serious crime during the mid-1960s. It was great fun; I loved the danger of it all. It was a great time. I had no qualms but I hasten to add that in all that period and in all truth, I never physically hurt anyone.

But of course, being a criminal can only end, inevitably, in imprisonment when your luck finally runs out. Why did I take this path? It was like a drug to me: the thrill, the spills but more importantly, THE MONEY.

After the pauper's existence of my early life, I simply wanted the best that money could buy. I had the best of 'Mod' clothing, the best mod scooters in South London, I was king of the pile but alas, it all came to an end in 1968 when I was arrested for safecracking. I was grassed up by my two accomplices, Vince and Borley, taken to the cells in Woolwich nick and beaten up by six hairy coppers, until I admitted it.

I served time in prison. Being locked up was like a living death to me. The sheer and utter boredom, the low lives of the inmates, the constant bullshit of the prison officers.

I soon made a decision that I would cease all criminal activities upon release. I couldn't do 'bird' again, could not come to terms with incarceration; NEVER AGAIN.

On the day I was released from prison my old pals from the underworld were in a car outside. I walked away from them despite their exasperated shouts, hailed a cab to the station and took a train to my dear sister number two.

She welcomed me with open arms and I settled down for a month in the peaceful solitude of the English countryside. I walked in the local woods every day, planning my future.

One of the coppers at Woolwich nick told me there had been £5000 in the safe that we had almost cracked. With that knowledge and at that time, I cursed my luck but not now. That part of my life was over...

MANCHESTER

It was soon after this that, incredibly, my mother said that she was going to leave my father once again. She turned up at the home of Kitty and Paddy one Saturday and without further ado, packed my bits and pieces in my old, battered suitcase. Whilst she was packing, she told me that her and Mellintrop had been working for the past year and had saved a lot of money and that she had over £1000.

I said, "Mum, let's buy a house..." The thought of having our very own home filled me with excitement. I soon came down to earth when she said that we were going to live in Manchester. MANCHESTER? Fucking Manchester? Apparently, that was where my half-sister number one was, living with her husband. I literally could not believe it. Here we go again, would she never leave me in peace?

We went down the stairs and Mother went in search of Kitty. We found her in the backyard where Mother gave her some money and thanked her for looking after me. I kissed Aunt Kitty and said my goodbye for I was very fond of her. We left the house
and my pals Bernie and Keith were bearing down on me. Bernie looked at my old, battered suitcase and said, "Where are you goin' Mick?"

I said I was going away for a while whilst asking my mother for ten shillings. She gave me a ten-bob banknote and I gave it to Bernie who was astounded and thanked Mum profusely. I patted them on their backs for I was quite touched about leaving them. I gave them my batch of 'money-off' leaflets. It was about the time when leaflets were starting to be delivered to residents of the streets and us kids would take them from letter boxes where the leaflet had not been pushed right through. It was quite lucrative as Mr Jones, the grocer at the end of Michael Road would give us a penny each for every fourpenny coupon.

Mum and I made our way to Central London, stopped at a Lyon's tea shop and gormandised beef sandwiches and cakes. Mother had it all worked out, she knew the time of our train departure and already had the tickets to Manchester. There was no lingering with her: here today, gone tomorrow. It was something I admired about her, once she made her mind up then she would do it.

We staggered out of the tea shop with full bellies and made our way to the train station with ten minutes to spare. At a kiosk, she bought me a pile of comics to keep me occupied during the long train journey.

This was turning out to be something of an adventure despite my initial anger for being dragged away from Aunt Kitty's. A woman approached us on the platform with a young girl about my age. She asked Mother if she would chaperone the girl until we got to Manchester. In retrospect, it was extremely irresponsible of the woman to place the child in the care of a total stranger but that's how it was in that era, people were much more easy-going than the regimented police state we have today.

The girl and I soon broke the ice and played games and stuff. I let her read my comics until she became tired and fell asleep, stretched out on the seat. Mother placed a coat over her and told me to be quiet.

Shortly after this, I too fell asleep and woke up to find we were pulling into the Manchester station. We all climbed from the train and stood on the platform with Mum looking here and there with a worried expression. Eventually, a middle-aged couple approached us, all smiles with the little girl smiling back.

She ran up to the woman and they embraced. It turned out that the man and woman were uncle and aunt to the girl. The couple thanked my mother profusely and slowly walked away with the little girl between them, the child looking back at us and grinning.

That's how it was then, people had trust in each other. There was no paranoia about child abusers or the modern dangers associated with kids. It is a sorrowful, far cry to the eras of innocence.

I never forgot that little girl and I have often wondered what became of her as I travelled through life. Her name was Connie.

Mother and I took a cab to Garden Street in the district of Salford. Sister number one opened the front door to us and emitted a piercing scream, bent down and hugged me until I had no breath. We went inside the house to meet my sister's Manchester-born husband. Just like my Uncle Paddy Drummy, 'Ken' had the same booming voice as he welcomed us.

Plans were being made. I was to live with the family and my mother was going to rent an apartment on the other side of Manchester. "The posh part," laughed Ken. Apparently, they owed a month's rent. Mum peeled off a few notes from her thick wad of cash and said to Ken, "Pay that tomorrow." They thanked her and I could see it was a great weight off my sister's mind.

I slept that night, in a tiny bedroom thinking about the events of the day. Mother had mentioned my schooling and had plans to enrol me at the nearest school. I was enraged. I shouted that I would not go. "You're not going to dump me in school down here, if you do then I refuse to go."

Mother looked at dear sister number one who said to her, "Don't make him, Mum, he can stay here with me, he will be good company." Mum eventually agreed and I gave the thumbs up to my sister with a grin.

I soon made pals with the local kids. They were good kids who liked a laugh and, as with all working-class kids, were up to all sorts of skulduggery. We would travel across town to an apple orchard and scrump the big, juicy fruit. They were always goading me to talk, laughing at my cockney accent especially the girls in the gang, who would say, "Go on Mickey, tell us about London."

One lad in particular, named Ernie, was a special pal. We went everywhere, all over town, always on the lookout to make a crooked few bob. We would buy ten woodbine cigarettes and share them, receiving much comment from irate adults who objected to two kids smoking openly in the streets.

He introduced me to Old Trafford and the giants of Manchester United, which stayed with me throughout life. Since then, I have been a supporter of the red devils, man and boy.

I was also 'stalked' by a girl named Esther. She was about my age and used to gaze at me with her big, blue eyes. Esther would follow me everywhere and it got to the stage where I would peep out of the back yard door, to make sure she wasn't lurking and only then would I venture out. The poor kid was in love with this scrawny cockney urchin.

There was a backstreet bookmaker who would sit inside the terraced house by an open window and take the punter's bets, mine included. He always had massive crowds of punters. His henchmen would stand around him in case of trouble and by the left, they were a hard-looking shower of herberts. I have always been a betting man and boy, my bets of a shilling each way were always paid out to me, correct to the penny when I happened to win.

On one memorable occasion, I backed three horses in a treble and all three horses won. I worked out that I had won two pounds and four shillings (£2.20). When I collected the winnings, Tom said to me in a serious tone, "I'll have to ban you lad, you take too much loot off me." He then burst out laughing along with his henchmen when they saw the concern on my face.

"Nay lad, only joking," he said, chuckling as he handed over my winnings. Two pounds and fourteen shillings (£2.70) — I had miscalculated the amount. Crook he might have been but Tom was always honest when paying out the winners; I never heard a bad word against him.

One day, Ernie called for me. I could see by his face that something was 'up'. We went to a semi-derelict house that was the meeting place for all us kids. Ernie turned to me and said, "I'm gonna nick a fookin 'tele'… we haven't got one at home but I'm gonna get one today. I want you to help me."

I stared at him and said, "How are we gonna do it Ern'. I'm not going to break into a house."

He shook his head impatiently… "Nah, we are going into town and I'll get it from a shop I know of. I've sussed it all."

This sounded like a right lark. I was always up for a spot of adventure so I agreed. We made our way to town and spent some time surveying an electrical shop, from a distance in the High Street.

I feel it necessary to mention that Ernie was as strong as an ox and about eighteen months older than me. We made our way over to the shop with Ernie repeatedly saying, "Got to get a fookin 'tele', got to get a fookin 'tele', got to get a fookin 'tele'."

It must be remembered that in those days of shop retailing, there were no security guards, no cameras and no chains locking the goods to the shelves.

Standing at the shop window and furtively looking

inside, Ernie said, "That's the bastard I'll have," and pointed to a television, the nearest one to the shop door.

Ernie said, "Keep the fookin' door open, I'm goin' in."

With no more ado, he pushed the door open and I grabbed it. In a flash, Ernie pulled the mains plug from the wall socket, grabbed the T.V. and bolted out. The proprietor yelled, "You little bastard," and vaulted over the shop counter. Instantaneously, I stuck my leg out and he crashed face down on the pavement. In a nano-second, I was off like a greyhound. I was a very fast runner in my young days before the smoking ruined my lungs.

I caught up with Ernie who was struggling under the weight of the bulky television which I grabbed off him. Still running, we turned in to an alley which Ernie had previously 'sussed out' as a hideout. We entered through the unlocked gate of a derelict shop. I put the ill-gotten gains on the ground, while Ernie collapsed and was laughing hysterically. I snarled a whisper in his ear, "For fuck's sake, keep quiet!"

He stopped laughing but giggled silently. Eventually, he got up and going to a corner in the yard, picked up a cardboard box that he had previously hidden. Ernie sure looked ahead when planning a 'job'.

We disguised the 'tele' somewhat. We stayed there until dark and then ventured out into the night. All was quiet on the High Street, with all the shops now shut for the night. Ernie carried the loot in its wraparound covering of cardboard. We caught a bus home and were soon surveying the goods in Ernie's house.

The T.V. was a fourteen-inch screen with the trade name of 'Sobell'. Ernie's dad offered me five shillings (twenty-five pence) for my part in the theft but I refused to take it. I said, "Buy a television ariel with that tomorrow."

There, it was done and dusted. If we had been caught, it would have certainly ended with our incarceration in a reform school. Anyway, what the hell, we had got away with it and the lesson I learnt was that, if you are determined and with daring, you stand every chance of success.

Ernie had never been to school which I envied greatly. I think he and his kin were Romany gypsies. Ernie was the salt of the earth.

A warm Autumn turned into November and boy, wasn't it cold? In all honesty, I had never been colder. Mother paid for a hundred weight of coal to be delivered to my sister's house and we would all gather round the roaring fire in the living room eating thick, buttered slices of bread and jam watching the twenty-one-inch television that Mother had bought for my sister.

One icy morning, the gang of kids called for me at the house and said they were going to make a guy for the age-old ritual of 'penny for the guy' (a form of begging) and would I help?

I said, "Bleedin' hell, it's freezing out there. Not likely, I'm not going out in that."

They asked if I had any gear or clothing to adorn the

guy so I gave them an old plastic football for a head along with an old, ragged top hat that my sister had bought at a jumble sale. The kids were well pleased with these items and went off with plans to build the guy. It was November 3rd and just two days were left to place the guy in a busy area and hopefully make some money.

I shivered as I closed the door behind them, having wished them well in their efforts to make a few bob.

Later that evening, there was knocking on the back door. My sister called out to me, "Mickey, it's your mates."

Silently I cursed, for I had been frowsting in front of the roaring fire thinking of the beef stew which was cooking in the kitchen, with a wonderful aroma that filled the house. Going to the door, I shuddered at the freezing air coming through it. I was surprised to see the whole gang of my mates, looking forlorn with a couple of the girls in tears. Ernie gave me the lowdown. It appears our gang had been attacked by some drunken, teenage youths who were all wearing the blue scarves of Manchester City football club. A few of our gang had been wearing the red and white scarves of the Manchester United football club. The Man. City yobs
had destroyed the guy, stamped flat the ragged top hat, ripped the clothes to shreds and kicked the push chair to pieces.

"Why the fuck did you wear Man. United scarves?"

"Are you all fucking stupid? "I said.

It appeared that our gang had received slaps to the face including a couple of our girls. Ernie had kicked one of them up the arse and had received a punch in the stomach, from which he was still suffering pain.

I called out to my sister if my pals could come in for a while, to which she readily said 'yes', having heard the sorry tale.

Sister sat them down and made hot, buttered toast and steaming mugs of tea. The poor buggers were frozen stiff. They had made the princely sum of three old pennies (about one and a quarter pence). But by the time they left, I had them laughing again, their cheery red faces lit up the dim room. There is nothing like the resilience of youth, down one minute and up the next. My pals, they were a great bunch...

Since that day I have always nursed a deep hatred of Manchester City football club and its heathen supporters.

When I was a teenager living in London, I would go to the London first division football grounds such as Arsenal, West Ham, Spurs etcetera and fight alongside the Cockneys against the City Fans. Yes, I have punched many heads of the Manchester City crowd. Revenge is sweet saith the Book and it most certainly is.

One morning in December, I was awoken from my sleep by sister number one. She spoke urgently whilst shoving my shoulder. "Mickey, you have a visitor downstairs, you must come quickly."

I arose from my pit and followed her downstairs. What came next was enough to stop me in my tracks and I was struck cold when I saw 'him' stretched out on the sofa. Yes, it was Mellintrop, my father; I was shocked and could barely believe it.

He dragged himself up into a sitting position, grinning at me and drunkenly said, "Hallo my lad, it's your old Da, come to see yer."

Oh fuck, why, why, why? I mentally cursed and went straight up the stairs and lay on the bed. I could hear his drunken voice drifting up through the dilapidated floorboards.

He was angry. "Jesus, if I had done dat to my old pa he would have given me a belting!"

I heard my sister placating the old rogue then all went quiet and I began to mull over what this would entail for Mother and me. It could only mean trouble when Mellintrop came to visit.

I started to become panicky and wondered what the future held for me. Jesus, why now after all this time? I lit a fag and sucked on it until it burnt my fingers.

Later on, my sister entered the bedroom. She said that she was going to see our mum and bring her back; it would take an hour or two.

She left the house and I ventured downstairs to see my father stretched out on the sofa fast asleep and his snoring shook the foundations. I sat opposite him, staring at his open mouth and wondering why he couldn't be like other fathers. He looked so vulnerable, lying there helpless.

I got up and went over to him. I placed my hands around his throat and squeezed them hard. For a moment or two, nothing happened, then all at once, he began to choke and jerk his head.

Of course, I could not go through with it and withdrew my hands from his throat. Luckily for me, he had not woken up and he lapsed back to sleep.

I cried silently, bewildered by the fact that I had wanted to kill him. I looked at the poor sod and whispered, "I'm sorry, Dad." I loved him, believe me, ALL I EVER WANTED was a normal life like other families had and my Da wouldn't give it to me.

I went upstairs to my bedroom to have another fag. I lit the cigarette and noticed that my hands were trembling. I was in shock at what I had tried to do. Stubbing out the cigarette, I lay on the bed and drifted off to sleep.

Sometime later, my sister awoke me to tell me that Mum was downstairs having a serious conversation with my dad and that I should go down.

I refused to go and sister shook her head resignedly. Laying on the bed, I began to wonder what the outcome of their 'conversation' would be for me.

By now, dusk had arrived and I decided to go down and find out what was in store. My father had gone out to the local pub and Mum was sitting on the settee. She gestured to me and I sat next to her. She told me that we would be going back to London in the near future but this time, it was on her terms and not my father's.

Then she astonished me by saying that I would be her number one priority and that I would always be with her and I would never be 'farmed out' to strangers again.

This, to me, was an unbelievable revelation. which

gave me tremendous relief. Now I had some real hope of a happy future. She said that most of the money that she had when going to Manchester was now almost gone. We were to leave for London in a few days' time with a short stay at sister number two in Essex, whilst mum looked for rental accommodation in Fulham. Dear old Fulham, the wanderer's return home together at last. Fucking hell. It was like being born again.

My sister, who had been in the kitchen, came into the room, her eyes red where she had been crying. She said, "I'm gonna miss you both but I'm going to get Ken to move to London. I just want to be near you." This was followed by more tears.

My mother consoled her and said that when the time came, she would help sis to find somewhere to live, in the smoke of London town.

My mum waited for my old man to return which he did a couple of hours later, as pissed as a newt. Then she went outside to find a cab which she did. She bundled my old man into the cab and made off to her apartment on the other side of town.

I went to bed that night in a delirium of joy. To live with my mother in a modicum of normality was all I had ever desired. The only fly in the ointment was that I had to leave Ernie and all my Manchester pals far behind me. I dreaded saying goodbye. Eventually, I fell asleep to dream of the old Battersea fun fair and my drunkard of a father.

My Aunt Kitty in Fulham had given my sister's address in Manchester to the old rogue, Mellintrop. No matter where my mother put down roots then Mellintrop would eventually discover where she had gone. He was a mystery, always disappearing, we never knew where he had been or what he had been up to. But this time, he had sworn to my mother that THIS TIME he would change — no more mysterious disappearances.

Later, in my life, I suspected he had a second family. Whatever the reason, he persisted in disappearing despite his oath to my mother.

Then came the day before our big trek back to old London and its yellow fog, all smoke and bronchitis. I had not told Ernie of my leaving or any of my pals. I just could not do it.

I gave my sister five shillings (twenty-five pence) which left me with one shilling and a few pennies, telling her to give the money to Ernie. I knew that he and his family were always skint, the cash would help them somewhat.

We left early in the morning, me, Mum, Mellintrop and my sister. Da was already drunk thanks to half a bottle of whisky which he repeatedly took from his pocket.

There was some kerfuffle when my old man said he had lost his train ticket. We searched him high and low but no ticket showed its green head. Eventually, my sister saw the ticket peeping out of the turn up of his trousers. He virtually collapsed with laughter and we angrily rounded on him. It was his idea of a joke, a craic the Irish would call it.

The long journey to sister number two was uneventful

but excruciatingly tedious. She made us welcome and had prepared for us. Mellintrop fell in a drunken sleep on the settee and did not rise until the next day.

Sister number two's family comprised of a husband and two small boys. Sleeping arrangements were a little makeshift with my mother sleeping with the smallest boy and me with the other of the brood. My da' was left to his own devices.

After a handsome dinner, I was falling asleep at the table and was quickly sent to bed.

The next day, I rose early after spending a rough night with the eldest of the boys. My sister said that our mother had got up earlier, with the intention of travelling to Fulham in search of rented accommodation. Mellintrop was still asleep with thunderous snoring. The boys giggled at the noise and the sight of him with his mouth wide open.

Mother returned in the late afternoon. To my joy, she had given a week's rental money for a bed sit in Fulham, complete with a separate kitchen. She said that I was to sleep in the kitchen on cushions taken from the settee. I didn't mind that; I had slept in far worse places. She also had news that I didn't want to hear. She had enrolled me into the local secondary school. This school, Henry Compton's, was very near to where we were going to live. I dreaded the thought of school but realised I could not get away from the fact that I had to attend.

We were to leave for Fulham the next day and I could not contain my excitement.

Mother left early on the 'morrow in order to clean

and prepare the flat for Mellintrop and me.

In the afternoon, me and he prepared to leave for Fulham and I said my goodbyes to sister number two and her boys. On the journey, dear old Da' stopped at a pub and stuck me outside with a glass of lemonade. The rogue spent the best part of an hour in the pub but at last came out, well 'steamed up'.

"Right boy o," he said, "let's go see your mother."

When we got there, Mother had prepared the room with fresh flowers on the table and a ham salad with all the extras. For once in my life, I was truly happy, eating and laughing at the antics of Mellintrop. We were like a proper family. We sat for ages at the dinner table, with Mother's splendid efforts at spring cleaning, all was wonderful. I remember wishing that it could always be like this. I was content and truly happy that night, never having felt like that for many years. The look of contented pleasure on Mother's face just added to my happiness.

PLEASE GOD DON'T TAKE IT AWAY.

Yes, that was my prayer that wonderful first night at the new address in Lillie Road but all too soon, it came crashing down about my ears. Mellintrop started his tricks. One time, he vanished for many weeks. Mother applied for National Assistance but was refused by that wonderful body of authority.

She had some help from a local grocer but only with limited credit. For a week, she and me lived on Kellogg's cornflakes and bread and margarine. I used to steal milk off doorsteps. Mum tired of this and got a job washing dishes in a hotel. She would come home late at night, totally worn out. She said there was much bullying in the kitchens of the hotel:

I fumed with frustrated anger and felt helpless. I could not do anything for her. Then suddenly, Mellintrop returned, chucking his money about but Mother's anger was awesome to see, she actually hit and slapped him. Needless to say, she packed in her job at the hotel, which was a relief to me.

I realised that this would always be the same, weeks of hardship with the odd spell of good times. I had to face up to it, there was no hope of a truly, happy life.

By now, I was thirteen years of age and the misery of the secondary school was hard to bear with its carpentry and metalwork classes, big, dark huts with hammering, banging and total crap, it was like a cacophony of hell.

I used to play truant a helluva lot and spend the afternoon watching horse racing on television, having placed my bets with the local butcher, a great bloke. My mother would nag me at first but came to realise that she now had no control over me.

The school was run along the lines of a borstal with rigid, harsh discipline. I received much severe punishment in the form of caning and a heavy rubber plimsole across the arse. This was dished out by a Mr Kitchen, the headmaster, mainly because of my fighting in the playground. You took your beatings in front of the whole assembled pupils and boy, did it hurt. I never showed my pain and that made old, cunt Kitchen worse.

As I said, the beatings I received were for fighting.

When you had the reputation of a hard-nut, every little arsehole wanted to take you on.

One day, that same sadist, Kitchen, hit me a blow with his open hand across the side of my head. His hand caught the air which blasted into my ear. The pain was unbearable and immediately struck me half deaf in that ear and has been ever since. All that aggro just because I talked in class.

I discovered two years ago, much later in life, that my eardrum was perforated on the side where that son-of-a-bitch had hit me. They would never get away with it nowadays with the modern liberal views throughout the schooling system and that's about fucking time.

I hated Kitchen and I often thought about handing out MY form of punishment TO HIM as a young adult of seventeen. Then one day, I read in a local newspaper that he had died in a car crash. The newspaper went on to say that 'he would be sorely missed' and praised him for his 'outstanding' teaching career. I had to laugh, if not, I would have cried. My one hope is that the cunt is burning in the pits of hell.

I owe the school one thing which I must relate before I close these pages on my early life. The local labour exchange had been robbed by an armed gang and a lot of money had been scattered in the street outside. The following day I had bunked off from classes at dinner time. I had to pass the employment exchange on the way home, when, lo and behold, I spotted a delicious five-pound note, partly obscured, in the gutter.

Yes, I picked up the handsome, blue bank note with its massive lion, it was a beauty of a five-pound note.

What a lovely god send. When I got home, I gave it to my mum and said, "You take half Mum and I'll take two pounds ten." (Two pounds fifty pence.) She was well pleased and patted me on the head. Later that day, I went back to the employment exchange and hunted every nook and cranny of the street but banknotes there were none.

Well, there you have it dear reader, my early life in black and white. Let me restate, that is how it was, in all truth. When I was fifteen, the official school leaving age, I obtained a job in a brewery, slave labour from 8 a.m. to 5 p.m. with Saturday mornings 8 a.m. until noon.

I paid two pounds five shillings for my board and lodging which left me two pounds to last the whole week. I had various poorly paid, dead-end jobs and it's no wonder I turned to a life of crime and then I was able to buy the finer things of life. I was not going to be exploited ever again.

Jacqueline, Mellintrop, my mother, my sisters, great aunt Gert, aunt Kitty and Paddy, Bernie and Keithy, Ernie and my pals of Manchester, Esther, Connie, Uncle Jamsey, Kenneth Parsons, Mr Joseph, Kitchen, the Lade family and Tom the bookie. They all lived again in these pages and they were both painful and just occasionally, happy to write about; sometimes I cried. I must say that it will be a relief for me to complete. Too many bad memories, too much pain. I am now just a sad, old fool, prone to weep at the drop of a hat.

CANCER PATIENT: Two Years On

The trauma and effects of radiotherapy hit me with a vengeance. Six weeks of intensive treatment left me with exhaustion and fatigue, the common ailments of exposure to radioactive substances.

The appointments were a nightmare, different times every day, sometimes 8.30 in the morning, at other times 4.30 p.m. It could be at any time and it was only the day before treatment that you discovered what the next day's appointment was. You could not make any plans for everyday activity. You have to live your life with the hospital at the forefront of your plans.

I used 'hospital transport' because it was free. That's all very well but many times I was late for the appointment because the cab or ambulance arrived late. It was the same when waiting for transport to take me home, it sometimes took anything up to ninety minutes of waiting before the transport arrived.

As I said, the whole episode was a total nightmare. On the other hand, the nurses at Guy's and St. Thomas' hospitals were angels personified, caring and sympathetic to your needs; total professionals all.

The last day of treatment was October 23rd 2015. Never have I been more relieved than when that ghastly treatment ceased.

On the night of October 23rd 2015 and after my last appointment, I crashed out in my warm and cosseting bed and slept for nigh-on forty-eight hours, my daughter supplying me with hot soup periodically. When on the third day, I arose from the bed with chronic fatigue and many side effects. My bowels would not work and I found it extremely difficult to piss, all due to the radioactive filth in my body.

But I thanked the gods that it was all over and looked forward to my next scan at the hospital to, hopefully, get the all clear from the doctors. In the past, a cancer nurse had told me that facial cancer was the easiest to cure; we will see.

Whilst I waited in trepidation for the proposed scan, my thoughts turned to keeping fit. I did exercise, rode a bicycle, walked the length of Queen's Road and into Peckham High Street. But with all that exercise performed while being drained by fatigue and sickness, I knew that I was unable to pursue exercising any longer. My body ached, I was consumed by nausea and in the depths of depression, I quit.

Almost immediately, I began to feel better, less tired and the nausea had ceased. Believe me, you cannot exercise when you have cancer, it just makes you feel far worse.

When I was diagnosed with cancer, I decided that no relatives or friends would be informed of my condition apart from my three marvellous daughters, Stephanie, Lucy and Caroline.

My eldest girl, Steph, moved in with me to care for

me, which she does to an unprecedented level. In all truth, I don't know how I would have coped without her.

The day of the scan approached ever closer and my stomach was performing cartwheels. My general practitioner referred me to various organisations such as: 'The Southwark Care Team', 'Saint Christopher's Hospice' etcetera. Despite the good intentions of these caring organisations, I refused them all. The more you succumb to care, the more you become reliant and ill; that is my opinion. I did not wish to be fussed over.

It was the day of the scan that would tell me either that I was cancer free or not. Because it was an important appointment, I took a minicab to Guy's hospital, not daring to use hospital transport in case I was late.

On arrival, I was told to take a seat. A man was sitting along with others, all with anxious faces. He held a string of beads in front of him as if he was offering it to some deity or god. His eyes were closed and he was mumbling prayers. I felt envious of him that he could have such faith.

After thirty minutes or so, I was called and thirty minutes later, I dressed and left the hospital heading for home. There, it was done, it was in the lap of the gods. An appointment was made for the following week for which I was on tenterhooks the whole time.

THE VERDICT

Waiting at Guy's on the day of the result of my scan, I became aware of an elderly couple, obviously man and wife, who had just arrived from within the inner sanctum.

The woman was weeping copious tears whilst the man was trying to comfort her. I heard the man saying, "Don't fret my dear, you heard what they said, I've every chance." His voice changed to a whisper as he lent forward, speaking in her ear.

The woman laughed out loud at what he whispered and said, "Ever the joker, aren't you sweetie?" The man smiled at her, they both got up from their chairs and left the room.

About fifteen minutes later, I was called by a nurse who studied my face with a certain sympathetic look as I walked up to her. Fucking hell, I thought, I'm on a bum steer here. She led me to a room in which there were two doctors. I was told to take a seat and then they both looked at me and did not speak. In those few moments, I knew that the treatment had not worked.

I said, "It's bad news, isn't it?"

One doctor then spoke. "I'm afraid it is bad news Mr Moran; you have a particularly aggressive form of cancer and the radiotherapy failed."

I knew it was a bummer when I first saw the nurse

with sympathy in her eyes. "I never had much luck in life, it's par for the course," I said.

The doctor went on to inform me that my nose would have to come off and that the doctor, who had not spoken, was the surgeon who would perform the operation. The surgeon said that, in time, they could build a prosthetic nose to replace the natural nose.

I had to sign various forms giving them permission to operate. Then I hurried out of that dreadful place and made my way home.

Naturally, I railed against God. Cursing and swearing at the injustice of life and thanking the Lord for kicking Mick Moran once again, right up the arse.

After a couple of days, I calmed down. Thinking seriously about it, that this bastard disease was eating me alive, made me all the more determined to fight it. I had always been a fighter and with the injustice I felt, I was consumed with hatred and burning rage at my suffering of this filthy disease. Total determination in taking it on, I was not going to die without a colossal battle.

The day of the operation came. I arose at 6 a.m. and, as requested by the nurse at Guy's, took a long bath. I had been informed by the medics not to eat and only to drink a little water. I took a cab to the hospital and arrived at 9 a.m. for the appointment at 9.30 a.m.

As with all the patients in the waiting area, I was called numerous times by nurses who asked a ton of questions whilst they filled out various forms which I had to sign. I became 'cheesed off' at all this and simply wanted them to carry out the butchery.

It was around 11.30 a.m. when at last I was called and told to change from my clothes into a hospital gown. Quite soon, I was being escorted down to the operating theatre. The nurses there were quite chatty in a combined effort to make me feel at ease, which I was. I just wanted them to get on with it. Then the anaesthetist said, "One little prick on your hand." I knew no more. I remember thinking later on, that's what it must be like when you die, booommph, you're dead and know no more. No dreams, just nothing.

I awoke that evening at around 6 p.m. It was as if a minute had passed since the knockout shot. I felt my facial area, it was covered by gauze but the hooter was definitely gone. Fuck, I never did like it anyway, bloody great snout that it was.

After a while, when I had fully recovered, a porter wheeled my bed up to a ward containing five other patients. It was bloody freezing cold in that depressing room with windows wide open. Crazy, it was bloody winter and I was in a bed right by the open windows. On my bed was one sheet and one thin blanket and I was bloody shivering. I hollered out, "Shut the bloody windows," which thankfully was done by a huge, male nurse, an Australian. And like all Aussies he was a belligerent bastard, moaning and grumbling as he performed the simple operation of closing the fucking windows.

I then asked for an extra blanket and he went off mumbling but eventually returned with the blanket. So straightaway, I had made an enemy in the ward.

The doctors came around the next day, going to each patient in turn. When they came to me, I asked one question which was all I was interested in. "When can I go home?"

They told me in one week's time, I thought, 'yeah, and the rest'. I was going to leave at the first opportunity.

Three days passed in the ward and I had just about had enough of life in Guy's hospital. Because of the removal of my top teeth, I found it impossible to chew any food that was hard and wouldn't you know it, every dinner was made up of hard substances. On the third day I made up my mind, I was going home. I drew the curtains and got dressed. Once I was back in my old clothes, I felt cheery once more.

As I gathered my bits and pieces, a nurse threw the curtains open and came to a halt when she saw me fully clothed. "I'm going home nurse," was all I said to her, as I stepped out into the ward.

She said earnestly, please could I wait for a few moments in the day room adjoining the wards. I said yes but insisted that I was going home.

Ten minutes later, a physiotherapist entered the dayroom and proceeded to instruct me on exercises I should do at home. Another nurse came in with forms I had to sign and then they both left.

Going down to the main hall at Guy's, I felt as free as a bird as I cheerfully telephoned for a cab. I WAS GOING HOME.

The wound in my nasal area had to be cleaned every day. I was supplied with gauze, tapes and quilted paper covers. My daughter Stephanie did the cleaning and application of gauze to my face and made a marvellous job of it, having gained experience in a care home. It was a tedious chore for her but she was always bright and cheerful about it.

Life went by easily enough but I was suffering great pain in the nasal area. I was prescribed morphine for the pain and found it to be a wonderful drug, an hour after taking a dose, the pain would disappear and I felt great. The trouble was I looked freakish with all the dressings on my face. Complete strangers would stop me in the street, as anyone could see that I had no nose. All the people were curious and sympathetic, I must say I did look an awful sight.

Then one day, I received a letter from Guy's stating I had an appointment in eight days' time: another scan was due. On the day in question, yet again, I made my way to Guy's hospital for the scan that was due.

The excellent nurses did their job and I left, went home feeling confident in the results of the scan.

A few days later, I heard from Guy's stating that 'as soon as possible' I should make another appointment. Now this sounded ominous to me, what now? What had they found now?

I arranged an appointment over the telephone for the coming Friday. Come the day, I saw the doctors at Guy's and it was as I feared, they had found cancer in my upper lip and top front gums. I knew beforehand that I was in for more trouble but I was still devastated when I knew, for certain, that the cancer was still poisoning my body.

The doctors said that the flesh removed would be replaced with flesh from my back. Apparently, it was going to be a seriously long operation and did I want to go ahead with it? I replied yes, what else could I do?

This operation was certainly long. I went under the knife on a Monday morning and only regained consciousness on the following Wednesday. There was this great wedge of flesh where my gums and lip had been. I must have looked an awful sight.

By now, I was heartedly sick of hospital life and I did the usual in discharging myself, which they were not happy with at the hospital. Another scan was due and I prayed that I would be clear of the disease.

Another day, another dollar and once again, I underwent the scan. Of course, the results of this scan were cancer positive, I now had cancer in the thyroid gland and it had to come out.

This horrible nightmare was endless but I told the doctors that after this operation, I would have no more of it and refused to have any more scans or operations.

I had the thyroid operation and two weeks later I had an interview with Dr Guerrero Urbano, the head of the cancer team at Guy's. When I told her that I would have no more treatment she said, "I quite understand, Mr Moran, you have been quite amazing."

I was touched by that and thanked her for all the help I had been given whilst I trod the hallowed portals of Guy's hospital.

It is now almost two years since the first sign that there was cancer within me. I have refused all further treatment and apart from the excruciating pain around the wounds in my face and, of course, the debilitating effects of radiation, I feel reasonably well.

It is surprising being close to death, how you become mellow and placid, putting up with annoyances and becoming generous, (the other day I gave a beggar a £5 note). You become calm and peaceful and less cynical about life in general.

Two years on I have my three beautiful daughters. I have my three wonderful grandchildren. What more can a sick, old man desire?

I cherish every new day that I stay alive, only those who live under the shadow of death know what I am saying. Two years on and fighting it all the way until eventually it takes me away…

THE ANTIQUE GAME

He loves a car boot sale
and the outrageous bargains to be had.
On the other hand
he pays the prices
that have his rivals
turning pale,
when he hands over
a bundle of twenty-pound notes
to make a tenner profit.
They say he is blessed
with good fortune
but it's not just luck,
although that plays its part.
It is fifty years' experience
in antique dealing
that provides him
with big bucks.

Many times
he paid a pittance,
that netted thousands.
Make no mistake he
is the Daddy of all
car boot dealers,

not frightened to spend
large sums on antiques
of rare beauty that
come his way.
Is it a pound
or a fistful of tenners?
No matter, he will pay
To the chagrin of his rivals
who mumble words of malice,
mean and callous.
But he pays them no attention
as he holds aloft,
his five-pound silver chalice.

He will sell you anything
from his house
but it will be costly.
There are no bargains there;
he takes great delight
in emptying your wallet,
right down to the leather lining.

HAR,
HAR,
HAR.

END.

THE BEAUTY OF FINE ANTIQUES

I love my paintings:
oil and watercolours
which I have purchased over many years
from car boot sales, flea markets
etcetera.
I paid very little for them all.
One particular watercolour,
which was expensive at the time,
costing seventy-five pounds,
is of a shipwreck
and has a present value of
eight hundred to one thousand pounds.
But I won't sell it.
It has been admired
by many dealer friends,
some of whom
wanted to buy it.
I thank the gods
for my eye for the antique.
With my forthcoming death,
to my daughters I have left
instructions concerning the sale
of my antiques.
They will not be ripped off

by rogue dealers.

Beautiful art from the past but alas,
I will not see them any more,
Not where I am going.

ULTIMATE LOSER

I learned a lot
in my school days.
Not the usual learning of academia
but the low education of the criminal mind,
thieves, liars and cheats.

The seeds of criminality
were sown in my young head
to be reaped astronomically,
years later,
when becoming a young adult.

That threepenny cigarette
bought at a tobacconist's shop,
was the beginning
of a low life and learning
that the crooked way
of the world
was all that mattered,
so it seemed.

Now with a cancer
that is eating me alive,
I look back at my life

to the many thousands of
cigarettes I have smoked
over a sixty-year period
and my venture into crime
which ended with a spell
in prison.
I realise that I was the mug
and not those quiet, studious kids
who listened intently
to the herald:

I was the loser, the ultimate mug.
All I can do now is a hopeless shrug.

BIRD SONG FOR JANE

She says
she can hear bird song
in her head.
Now, this is all well and good
but it is late evening,
with the daylight long gone
and the night as black
as a witch's hat.
The birds have roosted
high in the treetops, asleep.
I remained silent.

She says
the bird song is as loud and clear
as a tumbling 'mountain stream'. Her words,
with occasional multi-bird song, until
they are silenced
by a single blackbird who sings
alone and unopposed, majestic,
emitting a song of 'towering beauty' — her words.

She says
she wants others to hear it,
she wants others to share it.

She says
the singing occurs
only at night, never during the day.

She says
the wonderful sounds
make her feel warm,
peaceful and happy.

I wish that I could hear it
but it is not meant for
a two-bob low life
like me.
I would never be allowed to hear it.
It is only for those
who are spiritually pure
and innocent
with none of the vices
of the human race.

She says
she hopes I believe her,
which, of course, I do.
I reply, "Yes darling,
I fully believe you."

She sleeps now,
her hair as black as jet,
spread on the pillow
like a fan

and the full moon
shines on her hair,
the light peeping
through a chink
in the curtains.

"Are they with you now?"
I speak softly.
"Are the songbirds with you now?"

I am blessed
through this dying child.
Blessed because her pure innocence
and gentle nature
has rubbed off on me
and now,
I don't loath mankind as I used to.
She was instrumental
in bestowing peace in me.

I tiptoed from the bedroom,
leaving our little girl
sleeping peacefully and
did not weep
until I closed her door.

This brave girl,
this strange, little girl
who has angels
in her head.

JANE AND DELORES

I met Dolores
when I was just eighteen.
She worked as a barmaid
in a Blackheath pub
and was twenty-nine. Yes, she had seen it all and
yes, a large age difference
but I cared not a jot.

She had a daughter
from a previous marriage.
This girl's name was Jane;
a wise and articulate
child of ten who had been struck down with terminal
cancer and
was riddled with it,
with no hope and had
six months to live.

I devoted all my time to her and
we played many games
including chess.
I used to let her win
but soon came to realise
she did not need help

and I would put up
staunch resistance but to no avail.
She won all the games, you know.
Chess, I never beat her, not once.
I grew to love her dearly
and did my utmost
to be a father to her.

Soon, she could no longer walk
So, I bought her a state-of-the-art wheelchair
and I would push her to Greenwich Park,
where she knew the names
of all the birds and
all the names of the flowers.
She, in fact, educated me.
What a gifted child this was
but the spectre of death
was with us all the time.

I lived with them
for about eight months
and tried to be
a family man to
Jane and Dolores
but as the weeks went by,
Jane grew weaker and weaker.
I began to realise
that I could not face the death
of that enigmatic and courageous
little girl and simply

could not take
the sheer heartache of parting with her.

How cruel is this fucking world
to end the life
of a sweet innocent child
whilst monsters roam the streets
cheating, lying and are the cause
of unending aggression and trouble?

The time came when I realised
that I had to leave.
I could not face Jane any more because of
my near tears and choking voice.
Oh, reader, don't condemn me.
I was too young to face
the horrors of life
and the responsibility
of being an adult.
Here was I, a supposed hard-nut,
about to leave them both.
I guess I am just a coward at heart.

I left some money and a letter
for Dolores. I wrote a difficult
letter for little Jane,
asking her forgiveness
for leaving her and why I was leaving.
I told her I would always love her.

I quietly left the flat
and made my way
to the train station.
It was a bitterly cold night,
to add to the horror of my action.
I entered the station.
Hot tears ran down my face
onto the frosted ground of the platform.

I waited for the train
to take me far away
from my beloved ones.
It came and I was gone.

After all these years,
I still pray for them both;
still pray they are at peace.
I cherish the memories
of happy times and my little girl's
chatter and laughter.
So be it… I will always
pray for them until
the gods decide
to take me also,
from this earth…

WHEN HE OPENS HIS DOOR

It is coming on
to winter once more here,
in early October, the month that
finally murders
the sun and its warmth.

The herald of winter chuckles
and promises nothing
but relentless cold,
frosts, ice and
perhaps snow.

No more wild parties
in the multi-coloured,
flowery garden
at nine p.m.,
just darkness
at four p.m.
The heating is switched on
to combat the cancerous cold
that grips this diseased body.

It is a long way to go
'til summer is here once more. Honestly, I don't think I

can make it
through yet another crushing winter;
the prospect fills me
with depressing, black dread.

Half the planet in darkness
with millions cold and shivering,
pining for the sun
with its life-giving spears,
to warm the earth
and the people on it.

We must wait and wait,
it's a long way off. I
wait, for the gift from God
to warm us once more
when, once again, he opens his door.

SMOKE AND BE HAPPY

I have smoked cigarettes for most of my life.
Decades ago,
my mother, when potless,
would send me out
on the streets to look
for the public's cast-off dogends.
She would extract the
leftover tobacco from the butts
and roll it up
in cigarette papers.

Unbeknown by her,
I would steal one or two ciggies,
which initially
made my lungs somewhat sore
but I soon became a seasoned smoker,
enjoying the effects of the brown weed.

By the time I reached eleven years of age,
I was thoroughly hooked on tobacco,
spending my
ill-gotten money from a life on the streets
on packets of twenty fagaroonys.
In those days,

you could make a
a few bob on the streets
easily enough, whilst
most tobacconists thought
nothing of selling cigarettes to a kid.

In my teenage years,
I played amateur football,
park football.
During half-time,
I would light up a ciggy
in the dressing room,
much to the consternation
of the manager.

I did not care.
Having a cigarette at the break
helped me play better
during the second half.

When I was diagnosed
with cancer in 2015,
the doctors would berate me
for smoking,
which they obviously discovered
by the many blood tests
that I had.
I told them straight
that I would not stop
and would continue to smoke.

After a while,
they stopped nagging
and accepted the fact
that I would not cease smoking.

Throughout my pre-cancer life,
I always promised myself
that if I ever contracted the big 'C',
then I would still smoke and
carry on
as if everything in my life
was fine and dandy.
I had too many friends and relations
who, when diagnosed with
the filthy disease, cry out,
"Oh God, I'm going to die,"
take to their beds and
within six months
they are dead.
The medics say
that I should have died
three years ago.
There you are then. By living my life
as in my pre-cancer years,
I have survived long after
I was condemned
to two years of life,
which has stretched
to five years in total.

I have always been a fighter,
I won't give in that easily.
If you have cancer
I say to you:
"fight it all the way
and don't be frightened.
It wants you to be scared of it —
in that way it can
accelerate your death."
The holes and wounds
on my face are increasing
but I laugh at it,
I will NOT give in.

Every morning I awake
and bless the dawn,
another day of life,
I have survived the night.

Three years ago, my thyroid gland
was removed.
It was then that I informed
the medics that I was not
taking any more treatment,
no more appointments,
no more scans,
no more operations,
no more jabbing needles,
NO MORE.

I continue to smoke
twenty roll-ups fags every day.
I must admit that
these days I am coughing up
a large amount of phlegm
but that only reminds me,
I must go round the local shop
and get my ciggys:
TWENTY CANCER-TIPPED PLEASE.

CANCER AND THE PIT OF DESPAIR

This black depression upon me
heralds the arrival
of coming death,
whether it be
by my own hands
or the irrepressible
tentacles of this filthy disease,
of which I have suffered
for five years.

Now that the cancer
has almost triumphed
in this mighty battle,
all-consuming depression
is with me permanently,
day and night,
ceaseless,

even dreams in my sleep
are horrific.

On occasions,
I sit weeping
like a child

and an overriding
sense of hopelessness.
PLEASE DOCTOR PLEASE
give me a happy tablet
that would, at least,
help me forget
this scourge of depression.
Just give me a little joy
to remind me of
how wonderful
life used to be.

But the medical men
refuse to do this
so, I am condemned to suffer
until the end finally arrives
and I am released
from this existence
and the hellish black pit
of the manic depressive.

BONNIE SCOTLAND

The Scots
are a strange race.
Every Scotsman
I have ever encountered
has been aggressive
and exceptionally rude.

They have no love of the English
and fervently believe
that they are superior,
to all that is South
of the border.

When the Independence Referendum was held,
I bet good money
that the Scots would vote
for independence from the U.K.
I lost a packet of cash on the outcome
and was truly astounded
at the result of the vote.

For all their belligerence
towards the Anglo-Saxon,
they cling to the skirts of England

and its Welfare Benefit pay-outs
to the workshy, to the druggies,
and the drunkard s
of 'bonnie' Scotland.

The burden of the English are JOCKA ROONEYS.

A BRIEF MOMENT OF FREEDOM

At this very moment in time
at two a.m. on a summer's early morn
and after two spliffs and
after fighting for five years
in my battle
with progressive facial cancer,
I can say,
in all honesty, that I feel
in excellent spirits.

The black depression has lifted,
the severe facial wounds,
which usually are excruciatingly painful,
have gone, thanks to an extra dose of morphine. The
nausea and bloated stomach
are no more
and the relentless migraine headache
has disappeared.

These peaceful and pain-free moments
are rare events indeed.
Generally, I have the above ailments
with me for most of the time
and I thank the gods

for these scarce moments,
that grant me peace and sanity.
I find that I can write fluently.
I am without aggression, or pain,
my love of life returns,
so, I offer my thanks to the heavens
for this rare relief.
How wonderful to be happy
even if it is only for a short duration.
I think I will spoil myself
and roll another ciggy,
which has the comforting
touch of madam spliff.

CLINGING TO A SORT OF LIFE

With five years of cancer behind me,
one says and does little.
Minor activity reigns in this house.
The rooms need decorating,
the old stairs carpet that is worn and torn
requires attention.
The garden is abundant
with weeds and foxes abound,
looking
for scraps to eat —
which I sometimes throw out for them.
Either that
or they sleep securely
in the overgrown grass and weeds.

Christ, it's all I can do to put garbage
in the wheelie bin.
My time is mostly spent in staring out of
the windows' lace curtains at passers-by,
all with healthy, quick steps.
All have business to attend to.
Jesus, how staggeringly lucky they are,
although they don't know it;

taking it all for granted, as I used to.
Little do they know
that there is a sick, diseased, old man
observing them.

You know,
these lace curtains are alive
with features of a face,
monster faces.
Why is that?
Why is it only me who can see them?
Why me?

THE GREAT FARTING CONTEST AT SHITTON-ON-TEES

To fart or not to fart?
that be the question brothers.
On an old gravestone in Essex
was an epitaph that stated,
'Wherever you be
let your wind go free,
for it was wind
that killeth me.'
Adeborto Banjo.

This important question
concerning the breaking of wind
is universal.
The British treat it
like juveniles with guffaws
and much banter, like children,
PHEEARRUMPH!

The lower classes
hold farting contests
on building sites,
in factories etc.
Oh yeah brothers, believe me,

I speak from the experience
of such sad jests.

The French fart frequently,
not caring who they offend.
Now isn't that just typical
of the ignorant, froggy fiends?

On the other hand, the Americans
fart secretly and are devastated
when a 'silent' fart,
which they think they can get away with,
issues forth in a thunderclap
of a fart… PHEEEUMPH!

Fart, fart, fart,
Oh, to hell with it, here goes:
PEWHUMBBLOB…
Oh fuck, I've just stained
me pantaloons.
PHEWE@*?BLUBBLUB…
now I am disqualified,
Just like my life…

THE MIGHT OF MELANCHOLIA

The outstanding film,
directed by the talented John Schlesinger
was, without doubt,
'Midnight Cowboy' and won
a clutch of Oscars.

It cost me
some tears when, at the ending of it,
when the crippled,
long-suffering character of Ritzo,
after a lifetime of poverty and hardship,
escapes the winter of New York
in a Greyhound bus
bound for California,
only to die
as he reaches his goal.

I am damned
with this crying affliction,
concerning the hopelessness of mankind.
Fiction?
Yes, but it only reflects life in general.
So, I weep now and then
and try to hide it.

When I cannot hide it,
I leave the room
so 'they' cannot discover
what a soft bastard
I really am.

DEATH OF A CLOCK

My favourite antique clock
has given up the ghost;
a depressing shock, please don't mock.

'It keeps perfect time,'
I used to boast
to all and sundry.
Now it is toast.

Six calls to various repair bods
left me agog
at the estimates tendered,
the lowest cost quoted
AN ARM AND A LEG:
two hundred pounds, fucking 'eek.

There once was a man
whose repair costs were peanuts.
I used him repeatedly
but the poor bugger died.
I felt like shit,
I almost cried.

So here I am

with my darling old clock,
no matter how I scan the movement
and bestow a few knocks,
it refuses to work —
a fucking full stop.

I could easily pay
their costs of repair
but I refuse to give in
to the greed of mankind,
so, I remain desolate
without the mellow strike
of my beautiful timepiece;
my darling old clock.

FIVE YEARS OF CANCER AND COUNTING

I have long believed
that only those
who take the step to suicide,
enter a world
of peace and serenity
without all the detritus of worldly emotions;
'paradise' if you like.

We are put on Earth
as a test and only those
who commit suicide
are allowed to enter
the gates of 'Heaven',
for life on this planet
is the 'hell' that is written about
in the big Book
and those who are meek and mild
cannot live
in such a corrupt world,
with constant avarice,
greed, lying, cheating, murder.
A hopeless existence.

With this incurable disease,
I have had many thoughts
concerning suicide
but it takes mighty
courage which, alas,
I do not possess.

So, I will die naturally
and take whatever lies beyond with my
last bated breath.

WHERE IS THE POETRY DRUMMER?

I find myself listening
to the radio
more and more these days.
Classic FM to be precise.
No BBC rubbish for me:
BBC Radio 1 is aimed at the young
with its endless rock and pop crap.
BBC Radio 2 caters for
the mid-life brigade with
its mawkish easy listening/pop music.
BBC Radio 3 is aimed at the high brow
intelligentsia with obscure frenetic
'classical' music and la-de-da interviews
of the 'great and good'.
BBC Radio 4 is the home of
middle/upper class discussion
which is presented
by left-wing presenters,
with talking head stooges
who have far-left sympathies.

No, the biased BBC propaganda machine
is not for me.
I'll stick with Classic FM

and its wonderful crown jewels
of classical music, played
daily by professional presenters
with no politics.

You, dear reader, must think
what do the above words have
to do with poetry?
Forgive me.
I sat here for the past two hours
with pen and paper in hand,
seeking the poetry drummer
but try as I might, my
brain was shagged
so, I took the opportunity
to slag 'Auntie BBC',
the home of the politically correct
and biased posh hags.

DESPERATE ADDICT

The addict waits
for the telephone to ring,
drumming his fingers
on the coffee table.

His mood
is one of panic
with devastating, nagging, mental
anxiety, quite simply, manic, lurking
in mind and body.

He stares with hatred
at the silent telephone,
which he grasps
in both sweating hands.
Cursing, he throws it beside him
on the settee, knocking over
a glass of Red Bull
which had been precariously placed
on a silk cushion.

Even louder, he curses once more
and reaches for a duster
to mop it up when,

just then,
the telephone bursts into life.
Grabbing the phone,
he shouts into the mouthpiece
and gasps with relief
as he hears
the sober voice of his doctor.
Various blah blahing
doctor-spiel
and at last, he said,
"Mr Scrum-Pat,
I will give you a prescription this time
but you must
make the morphine
last for ten days."
Scrum-Pat hung up
and raced to the surgery.
It was with high elation that he pushed open
the GP's door,
grabbed the 'script'
and thence to the chemist
to obtain the drug.

On receiving the golden nectar,
he goes into the shop's toilet
and takes a long swig
of the morphine.
Sitting on the toilet,
he exhales in great relief
and begins to unwind,

letting the drug
run through his veins.

He sat on the toilet, eyes closed and
the confidence of life
began to relax him.

He sat there
for all of twenty minutes
and then,
calm and collected once more,
he left the pharmacy
and drove home
in his beautiful, yellow car.
All was great.
"Fuck them all,"
he laughed.
He entered his house and humming,
made a cup of tea.

No more nagging doctors.
No more lack of drugs
for a while at least and then,
after a week or so,
he would con the G.P
for more morphine.
But at this moment, he felt like
a tower of strength,
and all negative thoughts
were simply non-existent.

He fell asleep soundly and had
dreams of the gods.
Later, he awoke feeling warm
and elated.
It was like being born again,
a whole new chapter,
seventh heaven rapture.
Once again, he was alive,
until the next time. Oh God,
until the next time…

THE COLLECTIONS OF MOTHER

I came into this place, your
childhood home
and looked at
your mother's collection
of fountain pens,
liquors,
antiques,
postcards,
designer shoes,
photographs of her ex-husbands,
photographs of your ex-boyfriends,
then listened to
her collection
of sly words and I guess,
I knew then
that
like the dying summer,
you and I were doomed
for unlike you,
I cannot be collected.

THE REBEL

My old man would roll home
at night,
his drunken singing
ringing through
the tenement passageways,
after boozing it up
with his cronies in the Irish pubs of Fulham,
as pissed as a pudding…
par for the course…

He would rough me up a little. A poke here, a slap there
whilst all the while bellowing:
"Be a man. Stand up straight. Shoulders back."
It went on and on.
"I was in da Irish d'army at fourteen and a half,"
he would holler,
which was quite true
according to Mellintrop family history.

His father was shot dead
In Ireland in front
of him
in the 1930s.

Later, he would break down
sobbing, his tears dripping
on breadcrumbs scattered
on the wooden table,
crying for his father,

Later still,
my mother put him to bed,
his stentorian snoring
resounding around the bedsit,
his sleep of unconscious stupor.

A child can be shockingly resilient
at times.
I put a record on the turntable
and turned up the volume, knowing that nothing
would wake him.
I hummed along with the song,
not heeding about tomorrow
even though I knew, it would be a repetition perhaps, of
tonight.

He never, ever scared me.
The truth is, I understood him,
I felt his anger, I felt his pain.
He was my father,
if little else
and I loved him.

SANDRA JOAN

Sandra Joan will take your hand
and whisper that you own her,
she will summon you to another land
you go, for you crave to believe her.
She will lead you through
the blackest forest
until your cloak is torn like hers,
then lay you down in the river's mess;
Sandra Joan has made you hers.

The river's mud and I are one.
A hundred grinning faces
bid me welcome to my new home.
I twist and scream for Sandra Joan
but the ragged cloak is vanishing
and very soon is gone.
For Sandra Joan, the eternal search
goes on… and on… and on.

DWELLER OF TREES — ANONYMOUS

Distinguished Tree Dweller
of Jupiter's thoughts,
casting about in twilight remembrance
into the fracas of Blackbeard's seaport,
spurting iron words on the heads of old saints.

Distinguished Tree Dweller pouring pain from a teapot
over withered pubic hairs of an ancient harlot.
Delving deep in the annals of a long-forgotten sadist,
scholarly head, reverently bent,
lessons from a master rapist.

Distinguished Tree Dweller, conducting Satan's herd,
in De Sade's unpublished operas,
threshing in and out
of a mad man's poetry.
Searching for the mystic lost chord
to fit your ancient, rusted key.

The above was written to prove a point
to a 'new man' of the twenty-first century and his
pseudo-belief in such bullshit.
I wrote it in thirty-five minutes.
Pretentious tripe.
Get in the real world.

FROM THE BASEMENT

A cold day.
I am awakened
by a brass monkeys day.

There's Franey
with swelled belly,
goodbyeing husband, Terry —
the demolition navvy,
over my head
in the stars perhaps?
My car needs fixing,
but no money.
It's quiet now.
I cuddle the pillow
and return to sleep,
drifting gently away,
dreaming of E-Type jaguars…

I CANNOT STAND

I cannot stand
the cold of winter but then,
neither can I stand
the boiling heat of summer.

As a kid, after playing football
in the sun,
the blood would boil
inside my sweating,
aching head.

In winter,
I would sit frowsting,
in front of a fire
leaving my hardy, cockney pals
to the rigours of
football in the snow and ice.

This beggars the question:
is there anywhere in this world
where the temperature is a constant
seventy degrees? If there is, then
I would be off like a shot
to live there.

Fuck the blistering, toe-curling heat of summer
and fuck the pain of freezing bollocks wintertime.

Just leave me be in paradise
with a native girl in one hand
and a double whiskey in t'other.

A LESSON OF LIFE

The man next to me
at the funfair
stood up
and shoved his ball
into one hole,
when he should have
rolled it up.
He won the cuddly toy
through his cheating.
I would have won,
for I was almost
on the winning post but the rolling of the ball
was too long.
The lesson I learnt that day
was to cheat, lie and steal.
To do to those cocksuckers
just as they would do to you.

THAT'S THE STYLE

I believe she once told me,
"Smile at all troubles,"
So, we did.
I smiled even when she left.
Now everyone smiles
at me
and pass remarks such as,
"Good day, Mr Mellintrop",
"How are you, Mr Mellintrop?"
Even the man in the white coat
with the electric box smiles.
Tee-hee…

AVOID THE WORLD

I care about poetry, cancer and etcetera.
I write but is it good, bad or indifferent?
You, who perhaps like me, are averse to this modern world,
averse to news bulletins, averse to the
rampant monsters of advertising, 'Dream' cars,
fashion celebrities, politicians, pornography,
turds with legs, walking, breathing shite, that represents life in 2019;
nothing matters to them except material possession,
wealth, gastronomy, sex and hatred of his fellow man.

THE SLAUGHTER OF THE MIGHTY

The large picture
in the newspaper
showed a young man,
grinning inanely
at the camera.

He held a rifle
in his arms
and stood behind
the magnificent body
of a dead polar bear.
The report stated
that the man
was a 'trophy hunter'
and the dead bear,
with its beautiful fur,
was destined
to become a rug
in the man's penthouse
in London's West End.

In the name of God,
why are such enemies of this earth
allowed to live?
They should be struck dead

and their bodies burnt,
so there is nothing left of them.

Polar bears and elephants
are slaughtered
for parts of their wonderful bodies,
lions and tigers are murdered
for filthy barbarians to gormandise,
like pigs at a trough.

Such evil barbarity
exists everywhere,
be it wildlife
or abuse of children.

In the days when I was young
and only when justice fuelled me,
I was a playground and later,
a street fighter.
I was exceptional at it;
my furious rage would
guarantee victory most of the time.

Now, let me say,
'Just give me five minutes, alone,
with one of these fiends
who willingly perform acts
of such evil.'

Alas, there is

little justice
in this world,
for animals or mankind,
so, I must rant and rave
alone in my basement hideaway.
Cannot give help
in any way
to the oppressed
of this earth.
I must stop reading
newspapers
and cease watching
and listening
to the daily news.
It is too much to bear.

According to a long-dead
medical man,
I am a manic depressive;
which I knew anyway
and now cancer and old age
have me in their unforgiving grip.

I am so tired of this
cesspit of a life,
of heinous mankind
and all its trials and tribulations.

Fuck it all;
just pass me the whiskey.

THE NOWHERE LAIR

I wander, content,
in the dream of Wordsworth,
the yellow rivers growing wild.
I seek to dismiss
a distant, low growling
but into view
rears a motorway file.

Beset with media advertising
on television and radio,
I smash the mute buttons
and wait for a more important ring
from the antique dealer, Sutton.

He telephones:
"Could I bring the gear to him?
as he has 'injured his leg'"
Fucking liar,
he is just a lazy bastard. I've known him to pitifully beg
to save him making the journey.
That classic jaguar of his goes nowhere,
he is too scared to drive it.

So, I set off on the tedious journey

to Essex, by train and bus
and hope he is
feeling generous.
My bag is full
of all things antique
but he is not only
tight with money,
he is also a boring bastard.

Business over with Sutton.
He was quite generous,
right on the button
and he keeps a fine cellar
beset with fine wines.
All in all, a satisfactory outcome,
worth all the hassle of public transport.

Station, home, night,
I enter a turmoil:
a host of boots and fists,
are at war,
the red and white
over the blue
takes its toll
and one final surge,
see the blue are no more.

I enter my grim flat
and flop in a chair.
I am tired of the continuous

chase of life,
so much strife;
what is the point of it all?
I look at yesterday's paper,
at the grimy sink;
a complete and utter nowhere lair.

THE JOY AND EVENTUAL SORROW OF OWNING THE ANTIQUE

I own a bronze, scantily-clad figure
of a dancing girl
on a marble base.
Her hair is arranged
in a tumult of curls.
She is slim, lithe
and full of wonderous grace.

She stood on a window ledge
in a 'house contents' sale.
The owner, called Reg,
said she was priced at five pounds.
I grabbed it and passed over
the cash, knowing a healthy profit
could not fail, for she was
an exquisite figure
of the Art Deco period.

She stands in my house.
I could never bring myself
to sell her,
such was her beauty.
She has been with me

with every move of house
which covers forty years.

And now, with my death
fast approaching,
I look to sell her
along with other antiques,
for I am only their custodian
for future generations,
as are all collectors of fine art
and they too, are
destined to eventually sell and die.

THE YEAR GIRL

We met in January
when icicles drip from the trees,
when birds are famished
and frantically eat from
the bird table
in the garden.

She laughed with me.
In the sun,
when May creates love;
easily won.

In July, she said
she would marry me
but she dallied
and somehow, I knew
it was not meant to be.

Her laughing voice grew sober,
in the uncertain days of October.
I am alone now
in swirling snow,
as December's winds
do blow.

Nature prised her from me.

She said she would return
before spring arrived
but I knew
that was unlikely.
No tidal flow
will return her to me.

Nature stole her away
to sun baked shores.
She refused to stay and left
before deep winter arrives,
with its hungry jaws.

And me? Now with a blanket of snow
and the vicious winds of December
so hard in their blow.
They cut me in half and make me so slow.
So, she has gone
and it has to be winter,
my hated old foe
with its constant gloom and ice that splinters.

I sit by the window
and watch the kids
throwing snowballs at grandad Sid.
And so, I wait,
wishing the months away,

waiting for my half
of the planet
to be warm once more.
It is the god's gift of the sun
bestowed to the earth.
To massage my aching, weary bones.
I am wishing,
I am watching,
I am waiting.

A SICK MAN'S HOURS

My sitting room is an important and necessary haven for me.
I am surrounded
by things that I love and cherish:
my antiques,
my period bookcase and leather-bound books inside,
my vintage toys. Dinkys and tin minic toys.
Pre-and post WW2 and a multitude of collectable curios.

With my illness draining me of serious effort and strength,
sometimes I sit here for hours
just observing my possessions
and the cost when I purchased them.
Oh! the bargains I've had.
Some of high profit, some of small
but it's not the monetary aspect
I covet, no. It is the consummate skill
and craftmanship of man's ingenuity in creating art
that intrigues me, because my hands are useless
tools. They tremble so much, like leaves hang from
trees, in the cold but gentle breeze.

When I tire of this,

I gaze out of the window
to the tree
astride my house.
I spend hours until the format of the leaves
starts producing faces,
definite FACES, I see dozens
of faces. They bob up and down
and from side to side
in the autumn wind
and parts of them move,
as if they were talking.
It is a strange phenomenon.

I look each day
to see if they've changed,
to see if they've fallen or rearranged
and am pleased when I see
a favourite face, gently bobbing,
that the night has not taken.

You might say I should
'get a life', as the trendies would put it
but the cancer
rules my life
and my illness
confines me
to my antiques and that glorious tree.
For me, these simple things are a soothing comfort
and one which I never knew
before this filthy disease
entered my body.

THIS CORRUPT PLANET

The prophet of doom
came through the door,
a brown job
with the logo of: TFL,
i.e., the dreaded Transport for London.

With much apprehension,
I tore it open
and gasped in disbelief
at the letter inside.

Pictured, was my darling old Toyota MR2,
stationary at a set of traffic lights.
'Dear Mr Moran,'
it began and went on to say
that my car was releasing
high emissions
into the atmosphere
and carried a fine of £130.
WHAT?
You fucking, lying bastards,
thieves and con-artists,
duping the public
in order to enrich

the bulging council coffers,
whilst blaming
the 'wicked' Tory cuts
for everything
that these crooks can dream up.

The test of a vehicle's emissions
is a lengthy test
at a garage,
with a measuring meter
stuck up the vehicle's exhaust system.

The council conmen
had targeted my car,
simply because it has
an old registration number plate.

I contested the £130 fine
and, of course, won the case.

I would advise any poor sod
who receives such a missive
to contest it. Remember,
T.F.L are crooks;
they just want to get
their hands in your pocket.

MUSIC AND POETRY IS OF THE GODS

The construction of a poem
is similar to the construction
of composed classical music.
Both take time in the process,
images of delight
or sadness, of heroic content
or pretentious rubbish
or simply
crowned genius.

Tchaikovsky's Fifth symphony —
forty minutes in length
is a monumental piece
of triumph, overshadowed
by just a few moments
of mediocrity.

It is the same with poetry.
A piece of poetry
will occasionally
reduce one to tears,
with its beauty
or melancholia
but none-the-less,

may include a careless
choice of the odd passage or word.

The poem that really goaded
my tear ducts when I was
a child, step forward:
'Meg Merrilees'
written by
the gentle and ultimately tragic
John Keats.
It was the first poem
that ever spoke to me
as a kid,
every line simple but stark,
bringing images into my head.

POEMS? CLASSICAL MUSIC?
Thank the Gods for both.
The superlative music of
'The Warsaw Concerto'
composed by Richard Addinsell
for the 1941 film 'Dangerous Moonlight'
is, in whole, perfect.
The film's producers approached the
'top' composer of the day:
'Rachmaninov', to write
the score for the film.
He declined, below him perhaps? Tut-tut.
So, it was offered to Addinsell.
He was told

to make the music
in the form of Rachmaninov's style.
Quite simply, that is exactly
what he accomplished.
A truly magnificent work
that, once heard, is never forgotten.
It is by far greater
than anything Rachmaninov
ever scored.

ANTIQUES, TRULY THE LAST REFUGE OF THE SCOUNDREL

His junk shop was on
Lewisham Way, South London.
The proprietor was 'Joe',
a short-sighted, son of a bitch
with horn-rimmed glasses
with great, thick lenses.
He cleared houses
of the contents of the deceased
and, like all such 'clearance specialists',
was as sly and cunning
as a lorry load of monkeys.

I called just as he
and his henchmen had
unloaded the Luton van,
with all the latest goodies in boxes,
standing on the pavement.
'Joe', when examining an item
you had found
would hold it two inches
from his eyes and spend
two to three minutes going over it,
making sure he was not

about to sell you
the crown jewels.
Generally, his prices were sky high
and one would only be able to afford those items in
which he had no knowledge
of their true value. As I said,
a right son of a greedy bitch.
Occasionally, he would turn up
at his shop
in his Rolls Royce
and I was told by
a staff member of the shop,
that he lived
in an eighteenth-century house in Kent.

Well, good luck to him
I would say but for the fact
that he was a profoundly
greedy, miserable specimen
of the human race, who
would scream abuse
at his staff
for some minor misdemeanour.
I never, ever saw the man smile.

Well, on the day of his fresh clearance,
I proceeded to examine the contents
of the boxes with the man himself
and his bulging eyeballs
standing over me, watching me,

the paranoid bastard.
Just as I found a lovely
art-deco scent bottle with stopper
and very faintly marked: 'LALIQUE'
on the base, he was called
to the shop by one of his men.
I turned my back to the shop and
kneeling down, slipped the deco scent
into the inside pocket of my jacket.
'Joe' came out of the shop
instantaneously and for a moment,
I thought he had rumbled me
but was relieved when he
started to examine items
inside the boxes.
I walked to my car parked nearby
and looked back at Joe unpacking the boxes.
If I had been honest
and produced it to him
and if he had seen
the magic word of 'Lalique',
then the price would have been
'up in the clouds'.

Two weeks later,
I went to Christies at South Kensington
with various antiques, including
the art-deco scent bottle
that I had pinched from Joe.
I had a result with a Leica Camera

and then I produced the scent
and waited for the specialist
to venture from
the inner sanctum.
Eventually, he arrived
puffing and panting.
He examined the bottle
going all over it,
paying particular attention to the base.
He then spoke:
"No, it is not Lalique
but it's a fine representation
of the art deco period,"
and then he astonished me
by offering me £30 for it.
My neck hairs bristled with suspicion.
I knew that if it was not Lalique
then its value was around a fiver.
The old Etonian with the cultured
voice of Prince Charles,
was staring at me
and with a nonchalant manner,
placed the scent back on the counter
as if it was a stinking turd.
Do you know,
I wanted to head-butt him?
But instead, very softly,
called him a crafty cunt.
He said nothing,
turned on his heel

and returned
to the inner sanctum.
I did not 'grass' on him
to his superiors, after all,
I was as crooked as he
and would not inform on anyone.

I knew now that
the bottle was definitely Lalique,
so, I left the hallowed premises
of Christies' and drove over
to Bond Street and the
premises of Phillip's auctioneers.

Finding a parking spot
was a nightmare.
After thirty-odd minutes of driving around,
I, at last, managed to
find an empty bay.

In Phillip's, I was told
that the scent bottle
was Lalique and was
originally designed for
the perfume company of Coty
and worth around two hundred pounds. *c*
It sold at a Phillips' auction,
two months later for one hundred and fifty pounds.

This episode took place

around 1975.
Now, all the top-rated
auction houses only
accept items with a
minimum value of one thousand pounds.
Such is the affluent age
in which we now live.

The confrontation with
the 'old Etonian' at Christies'
actually did happen, in all truth.
I dealt only with Phillip's after
that incident and made
good money from then on
and would advise anyone
to visit them with their goodies,
for an honest appraise.
'Phillips' is now 'Bonhams'.

SOME YOU LOSE

The auctioneer sold a Lalique vase,
Ten kilograms of tobacco made it through customs,
A Rastafarian smoked another joint
and a Dunhill lighter actually worked,
while I placed another John Mayall album
on the vintage record player.
"Too bad," she said, about my losing bookie's bet.
"HAVE WE GOT MONEY TO BURN?" she shrieked.
Oh fuck, here we go again, more nagging.

I went out into the street.
A squirrel was limping on the pavement.
It would not last long with the street's many cats.
A neighbour hails,
"That fucking horse should be shot," he spat.
"Odd's on favourite and finished LAST?"
I sympathised. I had my money on the same nag.
"Can you lend me a score?" he asked plaintively.
I pleaded poverty, and could have lent it
but it would take weeks to have it repaid;
I know him of old.

I walked down to my vintage car,
a yellow Toyota MR2 sports job.

Seven strangers have asked if I want to sell it
during the three years I have owned it.
Chances are I might have to
but it would break my heart,
I love that car.

The sky grew darker.
I hate fucking winter.
She hailed me from the front door,
"Yer dinner is on the table."
I went in
but stopped as the limping squirrel
passed me, ignoring me, it was very ill.
I entered the house and closed the door.

A SUMMER'S DAY AT THE DINER

The man, sitting alone,
suddenly stood up
and jumped on the table.
"I'll fight anyone here, drunk or able,"
he bellowed and jumped down,
punching the air and stood: arms akimbo
in limbo, waiting for any takers
to his challenge.
Now, I had, of course,
heard of this type of incident
but usually, I would imagine, it's confined
to pubs when the challenger
is fuelled by alcohol.

He was obviously drunk or drugged-up.
I pitied him
but went on with my meal
with a dubious grin.

"Cunts," he cried,
drawing attention once more. Nobody wanted to fight.
The clientele carried on
as if he was not there.
I watched the man with interest

to see his next action.
He strode to the counter
and swung his arm across the surface.
Crash, bang, wallop. Glass breaking,
the remains of burgers, all were forsaken.

He grabbed a man's burger
and threw it at the staff,
who stood transfixed
behind the counter.
He looked all around
and then cockily sauntered
through the main door,
his muscles he flaunted.

The very young staff
began to clear up the mess.
Just another day's work,
their spirits to test.
I had finished my meal
and went outside.
To my surprise, there he was,
threatening an old man
who was trying to pacify
the oppressor.
As I walked quickly to them,
the S.O.B. hit the old man
who ran away to the car park.
as I reached the 'hard case',
I kicked him,

in his balls and he went down
like a sack of coal, on the ground.
I leaned over and looked at him,
doubled up,
holding his balls,
gasping a whining sound.
I knelt down and softly said,
"Go home you cunt,
it's time for bed."

Some of the staff came out
to applaud
and as I walked to my car,
I whistled a tune.
Nothing is better
than beating a prune…

BUYER BEWARE

The stack stereo system
he sold me
from his cesspit
of a basement flat,
is a fucking load of shit,
with half of it not working.
"No refunds Mick," he said cheerily.
Bastard. But the long and short of it is
we are friends.
He tends to my garden
in exchange for a twenty-pound note.
Now, I hate fucking gardening
so, I cannot afford
to fall out with him.

I placed the stack stereo
on the pavement in front of my yard.
Some poor sod will make off with it, hopefully.

I looked out after an hour,
sure enough, it was gone.
Perhaps they can repair it.
When Roy comes round
with something to sell,

I am going to be a tight bastard
until I get the money back
that I paid for the shit stereo.

Anyway, my old 1960s record player
has a far better tone
than these modern music machines.
I will put on the Stones' first album
and console myself
with music of the gods.

TO THE STARS

I am struck with an all-consuming fear
now that I am old
and diseased.
Normal, everyday life
bores me to the extreme
and sometimes I cry
at the profound
hopelessness of it all.

That I am near death
is the biggest horror.
What, for Christ's sake
lies beyond death…?
That is the question
mankind has been asking
ever since he first
arrived on earth.

Those who undergo
a near death experience
speak of a brilliant, white light,
comforting and warm
that engulf s them,
BUT WHAT IS BEYOND THAT?

When I was young and without fear,
I truly thought I would live forever
and hardly ever bowed
to obstacles in my way.
But as a child, I asked God to help me.
I yearned for a peaceful family life
which was non-existent and lasted until adulthood.
As a young man of proud confidence,
I blew away the past and replaced it
for a life of crime,
choosing high jinks
with the company of criminals,
never believing
I could be caught
but ah, the arrogance of youth.

The harshness of life
chisels away at you
until you are a shell:
empty and sick and aged.

Now, I just sit and wait for
the spectre of death
to arrive and end this misery.
All my hope lies
in that brilliant, white light…
Ad Astra?
Perhaps…

THE RACING ADDICT

Rasstus, he say:
"Where's that fucking form guide?"
Rasstus, you see,
is horse racing mad
and is addicted
to placing money
on bob-tailed nags.

His winnings are few,
his losses are high
so, he turns to robbery
to help him get by.
Just like a junkie
seeking the ultimate high,
the more the losing bet,
the more he will fret.

Rasstus cares not
of whom he hurts,
leaving his victims in a pool of blood
as from the scene he quickly spurts.

Rasstus, you are the devil's bait
and will never enter

those pearly gates.
Your brain will burst
for this is your fate,
down below where the fires are hot
they will burn your soul
and leave your bones to rot.

ODE TO MARMITE

Oh, thick, black gooey
tub of deliciousness,
I will eat you
'til the cows come home.
Lurpak butter on hot toast,
thickly daubed and with a little cress,
the ultimate test.
Will the boys love it
or drop it like a stone?
Love it or hate it,
or you cannot agree,
it's yours for the taking
for a small fee.

Its Desperate Dan's favourite,
It's in his cow pie.
Take a greedy bite
and your eyes will be lit
as the rich, beefy taste
produces a hit.
OH, MARMITE OF OLD,
my taste buds react
to eat you wholeheartedly
or just as a snack.
MARMITE RULES OKAY.

MANIC STREET PREACHER

I feel as though
I've been properly done
by the preacher
who had some fun
with a tannoy gun
screaming 'DAMNATION, HELLFIRE,
of the disease
that has hit the world.

He croaked the message:
"Mankind is on the path to hell
and God will show his wrath
by sounding the death knell
for those
who into evil fell."

I thought to myself,
what a miserable man
and how they must
love him at home
with his pessimistic belief
and his raging tone.

"We are doomed… DOOMED,"

he belted out
in a stentorian foam.
That's when I walked away
from his endless groan.

As I enter the door
of my peaceful home,
my thought was clear.
Tomorrow, for me,
a different path,
for he is in the same spot every day.
This path will take me away
from his fanatical stain
and cannot mess with my beleaguered brain.

DEAD OR ALIVE

Okay then, yes,
I admit it.
I am scared about dying.

I think about it now
for most of the time,
this eternal question:
what lies beyond death?
Just supposing one is dead
BUT your brain does not die,
the rest of your body
is toast but not your poor brain.
As they place your body
in the hearse, your brain
is screaming,
'I AM NOT DEAD,
NOT FUCKING DEAD.'

But, of course,
they do not hear you.
As the flames at the crematorium
burn you to ashes,
your mind
has just a few seconds to scream

at the unbelievable pain and then
you really are dead,
brain turned to ashes.
But what of the grave?
Your dead body is buried
along with your active brain,
which will operate for a
devastatingly long length of time
until it decomposes
but hell.
Just think of the
absolute terror you will suffer.
Actually dying.

It is those thoughts
that crowd my head.
Does not really affect me,
it's what comes after
that scares me shitless…
More tea vicar?

SHATTERED DREAMS

The publisher
sat on his chair,
flecks of grey
among black hair.
He looked at the writer
who squirmed
in his chair,
"I wish it was brighter,
too much gloom,"
he said to the writer.
"Take it away and more boom-boom-boom."

The writer left the room.
A year spent slogging
all for nothing,
no more typing,
no more midnight oil.

He knew the brush-off
when he saw it.
Untold publishers
he had seen,
one called it 'soft'
another 'mean'.

This publisher was number twelve and
at last, he knew
that he was finished, defeated.
He opened the lid of a company bin
and dropped the manuscript within.
He left the building
and sought a stiff gin,
with plans to visit
an employment exchange.
The bullet was bit;
life would now change.

As he walked down the street,
he began to whistle, a newfound relief...
It was over.
There would be no more grief.

ROY THE CON

The man from the provi'
was in a bit of a stew,
Roy won't pay back
the loan that is due…

Try as he might,
he cannot shift Roy
and is badly in plight
with his bosses on high.

The BIG boss calls at Roy's abode
and threatens court action.
Roy snarls, 'Fucking toad.'

He was taken to court.
He said he was not to blame
and pleaded INDUCEMENT.
The judge said the same.

Three pounds a month he has to pay.
He triumphed again,
at 12 bob a week
he suffers no pain.

If Roy owes you money
then take it from me,
you will wait forever,
so just let him be.

SEMI-CULTURED LOWLIFE

I am a toerag,
no doubt about that,
third class honours
for a first-class cad.

I spit the phlegm
brought up from within
into the waste bin.
My daughter is stunned,
"Let 'em recycle that,"
I say to my kin,
who wanders away
taking the bin.

I bathe, once in a while,
and pick the scabs
from the open wound
that is my face,
flicking them on the carpet,
I've absolutely no grace.

Given the opportunity,
I shoplift from stores
just for the hell of it,

over the loot, later I'll pore.

I will slap the next bore
who asks with a snigger,
"Where's your nose?"
The hole in my face:
"Will it get bigger?"

I spot a banknote
on the ground,
I place my bag over it,
fifty pound.
I stoop down
as if tying my shoelace,
then scooped the loot
into my bag;
with a puffed-out chest
this result is the best.

Long live car boot sales,
you never know what treasure awaits.
Be it buying or finding
but can be a blow
when someone beats you to that bargain.

On the other hand,
I am something
of a cultured, bad man.
I adore and sometimes weep
at classical music

that cuts so deep
into my ragged soul.

I make monthly payments
to the P.D.S.A. and
the Dog's Trust
because they deserve help,
the humans can cuss.

My brain has evolved
from Sun-type papers
and their flashing tits and
banal articles
by so-called wits.
I moved on long ago
to 'The Times'.
I enjoy the obituaries;
long may they shine.

But low life I am
with just a sprinkling
of culture.
A toerag and thief,
for sure a vulture.
Shitehawk I am
but with manners,
a Samaritan to the weak,
helpless and hopeless.

BLESSED ARE THE SMALL HOURS

Two in the morning
the street has died,
nothing moves,
there is no cry.
Houses in darkness
whilst the rippled sheen
of Victorian glass
shelters those within.
Lovers, kids, brothers and sisters,
nannies, dogs, cats and diamond geezers,
brother Jez
and his antique, red fez.

All life lies behind
these antique homes.
At two in the morn
I close the gate,
must mow the lawn...
mustn't be late,
tomorrow... perhaps.

A fox pads by
catching my eye.
He sees me

and quickens his pace,
scavenging for man's
cast away scraps,
bought earlier
from takeaway shacks.
Let him eat,
help him sniff out the meat.

I yawn, growing tired,
just one more fag
whilst I sit by the fire.

Night night,
my Jackie love.

A SHORT STAY DOWN UNDER

Don't hold your fag
in a certain way,
you will be considered
a raving gay
by certain members
of the lower-class.

Never let on
that you love the opera,
you will be considered
a demented poofter
by certain members
of the lower-class.

Never treat a man
with all due respect,
you will be considered
a poofter pest.

Living with these people
drove me down
to act the part
of a sad, old clown.

I soon took a plane
from whence I came,
back to old blighty
leaving Oz to its shame,
where the inhabitants
have queers on the brain.

CROOKS ALL

I switched on the ignition,
the beast's engine roars in response.
"Lovely motor mate,"
has been said many times.
They, complete strangers, have wanted to buy it.
It's nice to own something
that everyone else wants to own.
It's mine, its mine, the only car I ever coveted.

The yellow beast,
at great pace
tears down the street.
Its speed would make a police case
and get me into trouble,
one of these days.
I find it easy
to cheat speed cameras
but it's the hidden copper
with a speeding gun
that is liable to catch me out.
But the thrill of driving fast
far outweighs the threat of endorsement.
I have to give 'beast' her head
now and then. Everyone
wants her, loves her, this beast of a motor.

Nine Weeks Later…

The copper stepped out
from behind a hedge,
holding a speed gun
directed at my breast.
He ushered me onto
 a bit of rough,
off-road parking.
Fuck. Another three points
on my license.

I jumped out of the car
as the copper sidled up to me.
"My, my, my, we are in a hurry
aren't we sir?"
Typical copper's spiel.
Here goes nothing,
Its 'shit or bust', I thought.

I was going to 'try it on'.
On opening my wallet,
I pulled out my driving license
and a twenty-pound note
handing both to P.C. Plod.
He looked at them
then held the banknote
in the air and said:
"Are you offering me a bribe, sir?"
and spoke softly, the signs were good.

"Of course not, officer, no, no,
I want you to donate the money
to the Police Widow's Fund."
He looked at me
with dull eyes and placed
the £20 in his jacket pocket.
"Off you go sir and
in future, SLOW DOWN."
"Certainly, officer and thank you,"
I replied.
Jumping in the car,
I went down the road
only punching the air
in victory mode
when the cop was out of sight.
WOW. FUCKING ADA.
What a result.
I had something that night
to tell the boys

As I sped along
the road, I thought what a
wonderful country this is,
with its corrupt
police, bless them.

I patted the dashboard
of the beast and sang
'Jerusalem ', jeez,
I LOVE THIS
FUCKING CAR.

THE INDIGNITIES OF AN AGED CANCER SUFFERER

Kidney problems,
Bowel problems,
Hard to piss,
Flatulence,
Complete loss of smell,
Complete loss of taste,
Loss of appetite,
Loss of weight,
Sleeping excessively,
Aching bones,
Extreme fatigue,
Dribbling tea, coffee, all liquids,
No longer able to defend myself,
Cowardice,
Extreme reliance on others,
Reluctance to bathe,
Short-tempered,
Cannot tend the garden,
Bed sores,
Wound pain from operations,
Waking every day with headaches,
Slurred speech,
Thinking of hell,

Thinking of heaven,
Vision getting worse,
Falling over,
Trembling head and hands,
Impotence.

You, dear reader, who perhaps
is young and healthy,
promise me that
you will enjoy life.
For I did not
and I have this disease
to face up to.
For five years, I have fought it
and know it will kill me eventually.
I can look back
on too few good memories.
Perversely, I will welcome death.
I am curious you see
but I will still fight the filthy disease,
just as I have always fought
adversities.

A TIME-WASTING DAY OF THE BRITISH

Monday 10 a.m.
My car was broke,
alternator belt was broken
so said the RAC geezer.
I fired up the old computer
and found, through google,
a mobile mechanic
based near to me
in London.
I phoned the given number
and the well-spoken receptionist
asked many questions of me
regarding my car.
I rang off
after giving all the details,
expecting her to call back soon (she said).

Monday afternoon 3 p.m.
Nobody had contacted
so, I called the 'mobile mechanic'
once more but nobody picked up.
I persistently kept calling

up until 5 p.m. when I gave up.
A whole day had been wasted.

Tuesday morning 10 a.m.
I contacted a local garage
which was owned and run
by East Europeans who,
incredibly, came out to view the car
and then drove back to the garage
after giving the battery a small charge.
I must say that I was
somewhat uneasy about this
but I had to trust them.

Three hours later,
the head guy at the garage
phoned me to say
that THE CAR WAS REPAIRED.
I couldn't believe it
after the hassle of the previous day.
They had also replaced
the air conditioning belt
which had been missing.
He also said
that he would drive the car back to me
to save me the short walk.
All-in cost was ninety pounds.

So, my mistrust was unfounded,
they were great guys who

did not mess me around,
they go that extra mile,
getting me back on the road
in no time at all.

Those of you of a certain age
will remember the days of old
when the mainly
British shopkeepers worked until noon
on a Thursday:
half-day closing
they called it
and would also
close their shops at 5 p.m.
on other weekdays.

Now, you can shop 24/7
all hours, all over London,
welcome foreigners manning the tills.
Their workload puts the British
to downright shame.

One last word
on the 'mobile mechanic'.
I am frequently amazed
at adverts placed on the internet
where one is unable to get
to deal with dealers through
sheer incompetence or apathy.

I never did receive any
communication from the so-called
'mobile mechanic'.
He's probably got his feet up
on the desk and shouting
for another cup of tea.

Give me a foreigner to deal with
Any day.
They have an aptitude
for sheer, bloody, hard work
and deserve the cash they earn.

I am certain
the fucking internet
is the work
of the Devil.

Long live Bulgaria!

THE TOILET IS DOWN THE HALL VICAR

These cancerous holes
in my face,
beside the area of my missing nose,
have expanded drastically
and are heading
ever upwards
towards my eyes.

What is on the cards?
What will arrive first,
death or blindness?

I would rather death over blindness.
To lose your eyesight
is the end of your life.
The thought of total reliance
on others
frightens the crap
out of me.

The gods above
play with us, here on earth
issuing death

and disease on a whim.
For others, good fortune
and a long, long life.

I guess my misfortunes
are for the life
I have led.
I can almost smell the fumes
of the crematorium.
If I become blind then I have a stash
of sleeping pills
to end it all.

The toilet vicar?
You know where it is
but if it is a gigantic turd
like last time,
that would not flush,
then you can hook it out yourself…
KERRRUMPH…

THE ART TEACHER

We had a teacher
in secondary school.
His name was Mr Joseph.
Art was his subject
and the poor bugger
really tried to
educate us ignorant urchins.

He was a passive,
gentle and kind
teacher, who tried
to inject some culture
into a bunch of
piss-taking cockney kids.
He fought a long
and ultimately futile
battle with us,
never losing his temper,
never once using the cane or slipper.

One day, he brought in
a large and bulky
tape recorder and said
he was going to play

'The marriage of Figaro'
for us and would like
our views on it
at the end.
We listened with utter boredom
which ended in chaos
with the entire class,
me included, roaring out:
"Oi Figaro. Hey Figaro. Hey Figaro
Figaro you cunt.
Figaro, get off me mum."
Mozart would have
turned in his grave.
The hapless Mr Joseph
charged about the room
saying: "Who said that?
Be quiet, all of you,"
in his soft, gentle voice.
The din continued until
the dreaded figure of Mr Kitchen, the headmaster
entered the room.

At once there was
total silence with
Kitchen shouting:
"I will cane anyone
disrupting the class,"
and stalked out of
the room.

Later that day
during dinner hour,
two friends of mine,
Basel and Desmond
and me were aimlessly
wandering around the playground,
when we were accosted by Mr Joseph
who had a camera around his neck.
"I'm going to take a photo
of three idiots who are the bane of my life,
to show my family what I have
to put up with."
"Why not?" we said,
it was a bit of a lark.
So, we lined up displaying
V signs and sticking
our tongues out.

Mr Joseph eventually
produced the photograph
for us and Basil and Desmond
were laughing at it
but as for my own part;
I felt nothing but shame as I looked at three scumbags in
the picture.
I was sorry Sorry for the art teacher,
a thoroughly decent man,
too soft for the job.

I never 'played up' in

Mr Joseph's class again.

He must have died long ago
but I can still remember
every feature of his cultured face
and my remorse, at my own crass
behaviour and this leopard changed its spots, from that
moment on.

THE MOST BORING, FRUSTRATING AND HATEFUL THINGS ON THE PLANET

BOREDOM A politician's memoirs.
BOREDOM The night dreams of others.
BOREDOM Kiddies' school musicals.
BOREDOM Julie Andrews' films.
BOREDOM Ken Dodd's long-playing records.
BOREDOM A partner who doesn't talk.
BOREDOM 'Star Wars' films.
BOREDOM E.T. the film.
FRUSTRATING Running out of tobacco when the shops have closed.
HATE Jeremey Corbyn.
BOREDOM A car boot sale seller who gives you an account of his life.
BOREDOM The London marathon.
HATE Threats from a debt collection agency.
FRUSTRATING When your car refuses to start.
BOREDOM Jehovah's Witnesses.
HATE A rabid cold-caller who only wants to get his hand in your pocket.
BOREDOM The communal singing of 'Abide with me' at F.A. Cup finals.
BOREDOM Cocaine.

FRUSTRATING A watercolour painting that turns out to be a print.
BOREDOM Lesney matchbox toys.
HATE Mass media advertising.
BOREDOM The Times' obituaries of the high and mighty, politicians etc.
HATE A shop assistant with attitude.
BOREDOM The Life and Times of Huckleberry Finn.
FRUSTRATING A gardening book with black and white prints.
HATE Neighbours with 'boom-boom' stereo systems.
HATE Frenetic classical music.
FRUSTRATING Radio presenters who mumble and whisper.
FRUSTRATING DVDs with no sub-titles.
BOREDOM All T.V. programs apart from football and classical music.
HATE You travel forty miles to a field and your metal detector refuses to work.
BOREDOM Puzzle pages of puzzles in newspaper supplements.
BOREDOM Neighbours who accost you in the street and gabble on and on.

BOREDOM Publishers who won't acknowledge my genius, (tongue-in-cheek).
HATE High Street preachers with a deafening tannoy.
HATE All 'reality' T.V. I've never watched any of that crap.
HATE Opening modern retail packaging is like trying to

bust into Fort Knox.
BOREDOM Pot, grass, whatever, does little for me.
BOREDOM Growing a beard. I am too lethargic to shave but hate the hair.
HATE Chinese reproductions of antiques, they've copied everything.
BOREDOM The works of William Shakespeare, incomprehensible puke.
BOREDOM Pedigree lapdogs, give me a big, bouncing, boisterous mongrel every time.
FRUSTRATING Car boot sale sellers who come out without any small change.
HATE The Daily Mail, nothing in there but so-called 'celebrities'.
BOREDOM Any form of religion, it bores me to tears.
FRUSTRATING The mighty reds of Manchester United. I hate it when they lose.
HATE This sad, modern era that has given birth to the 'politically correct' brigade.
HATE Priests of high-power prostrating themselves over sins of two-hundred-year-old occurrence.
BOREDOM ? Having to roll a cigarette.
HATE The rabid left-winger spouting his views on communism.
HATE Manchester City football club who were unbeatable.
HATE Liverpool football club who are unbeatable.
FRUSTRATING A biro pen that won't work upside down.

FRUSTRATING An antique clock that refuses to work despite three hours toil.
HATE Cars that park two inches from your bumper.
FRUSTRATING Endless hospital appointments when you have cancer.
BOREDOM People of stunted growth with attitude problems.
HATE Security guards in shops who think they're in the SAS.
HATE Tapioca, semolina and warm milk.
HATE Downright lies by eBay sellers.
HATE Computer refusing to work.
BOREDOM Christmas.
BOREDOM New Year Holidays.
FRUSTRATING When your bet falls at the first fence in the Grand National.
BOREDOM Holidays abroad.
BOREDOM Endless waiting on a motorway multi pile-up.
HATE The froggy French who said to Hitler: "Come, take our Country."
HATE Councils who make millions of pounds in car fines and then blame '"the wicked government cuts'" for causing austerity.
BOREDOM The totally boring Morecambe and Wise 'comedians'.
HATE Morphine running out two days before it is due once more.
BOREDOM Singalonga Max.

HATE Pseudo white groups recording Negro R&B.
HATE Queers 'coming out' and admitting they are 'gay' in floods of tears.
FRUSTRATING Tower Bridge, why is it always raised when I use that route?
HATE The sly bastards at the BBC and their left-wing bias.
BOREDOM Harry and Megan, it will all end in tears for Harry.
HATE I would appreciate it if Jamie Carragher would take elocution lessons.
HATE Global warming, it does not exist.
FRUSTRATING A full moon when metal detecting at Silchester.
HATE The Thames Barrier holding in the low tide.
HATE Me.
HATE Myself.
HATE Mick Moran…Moronic Mick.
HATE The biggest bore of them all.

CORONA VIRUS

It is now seven months since the last
of the car boot sales.
This corona virus
or Covid-19,
call it what you will,
started in March 2020 and almost immediately,
large groups and gatherings were banned.
Hence,
the demise
of car boot sales.

I greatly miss
driving my handsome car
a few miles into
central London
where, every week,
my motor was much admired
and yet again, some posh gent
would want
to buy it.

I would proceed
to have glorious
purchases of all things, antique or collectible

and then,
joyfully return home,
laden down with potentially
great buys.

How I miss those sales.
Sunday was
the highlight of my week.
Now, who knows when
they will return,
if at all?
Already the Battersea events
established in 1999
have given up the ghost
and closed its gates for ever more.

'These things are sent to try us,'
so the big book tells us.
This 'thing' has certainly 'tried' me.
No more making money,
no more jocularity with
boot sale friends
and fellow dealers.

Will the virus
ever be defeated?
Perhaps not, maybe
it's the end of mankind.
It's going to take a long time
for it to be annihilated,

if that is ever achieved.

May be mankind
will eventually defeat it,
who knows?
So, at the moment,
the whole world
holds its breath and sweats.

Perhaps once again, the jolly event
of a car boot sale
will reappear.
The whole world waits
with bated breath,
for life to return to normality.

This hard used,
old planet called Earth
is host to the mad men
in the science labs,
who contaminate
the atmosphere
with their filthy poisons.
KERRUMPHEEE.
Another cake Vicar?

THE JAW-JAW OF ENGLAND

The British
would win
gold medals
galore,
if there were
Olympic categories
for talking more and more.
Waffle waffle,
jaw jaw,
hardly ever
reaching a
decision.
"Put it on
the back burner Olly,
we will discuss it
next year
or perhaps in
two years when we
are fit and jolly.
Not now, we have more important things to discuss."
than school dinner's for children of the poor
well that can wait,
the team will vote
for 200 bicycle lanes

for Peckham agreed
then?
A chorus bellow agreed.

I've reached
a decision.
I refuse
to indulge
in the
Queen's English.
That is, jaw jaw,
waffle waffle.
Too much
is said,
too much
is not ad-libbed,
just nonsensical,
time wasting rhetoric,
shouting, whisperin',
stentorian cacophony.
You know,
I could quite happily
be dumb, never
to speak again,
"Eh? What was that Olly?"
I would have a sign around my neck, DUMB.
Bye bye, Olly.

AWA WICH YER RABBIE

The receptionist at
the mail order company
said she was sorry
but the electronic
mouse repellent
was sold out. Now,
I cannot and refuse
to kill the poor little sods,
scrabbling about under
the floorboards trying
to keep warm,
in this unrelenting winter;
starving, starving,
only dust and rubble
down in the depths,
no food there.

So, they come up
into my kitchen
looking for crumbs and scraps.
The thing is,
they are undoubtedly vermin,
carrying all sorts
of germs, so,

we can't have that, can we?

I seal up the gaps
and holes around
the skirting boards,
breathing: "Please,
don't break these down again."

No electronic mouse repellent.
It would have been ideal,
keeping the poor buggers
at bay
and hoping that
they will move to a new house
and go next door.
These fucking mail order companies
are all the same,
always sold out
of the one thing
you desire.

There was this ancient 'poet'
named Rabbie Burns,
who called a mouse
'a wee, cowering, timorous beastie'.
Of course, the bloody mouse was scared
with a big, hairy, aggressive Jock
breathing whiskey fumes
on its little head.
A tiny mouse and a huge,

fat Jock towering over it.
Wouldn't anything/one be scared?

I sometimes think
I should become a 'Jaine',
whereby one doesn't hurt
the merest living being.

I even feel guilty
when killing a house fly;
even a fly.
But then human beings
come into the story
and in my life
I've physically hurt many
of mankind when they've deserved it
and I enjoyed it, so I
could not become a Jaine
because, even at my age,
I still enjoy my
rucks with mankind.

Go in peace,
little mite,
I will not hurt you.

And so, to bed.

AN ENCOUNTER WITH THE SUPERNATURAL

In the midst of my calamities,
you know, cancer
and all that goes with it,
I am being haunted
by a ghost/poltergeist
that lives in my bedroom.

It all started in 2017
when I awoke one morning
and found
curious occurrences
that had happened overnight.

My bedside table lamp
was on its side, lying
on the floor
next to my bed.
My shoes,
which I always leave beside my bed,
had been thrown in disarray,
in a far corner
of the room.
The computer had been switched on

and was tuned in to eBay.
One can understand
how I was totally perplexed
at these happenings;
the thought of ghosts
never entered my head.
I have always believed
that ghosts
and the supernatural
did not exist.
I questioned my daughter
thinking that she may have been
playing a prank on me
but she was genuinely puzzled,
just as I was.
By the time
I went to bed that night,
I had dismissed
the events of the morning
as a mystery that could not
be solved and went to bed.

I had been asleep for some time
when I was awoken by loud knocking
which emanated
from a wardrobe
on the far side of the room.
I jumped out of bed and
immediately,
the knocking ceased.

I went over to the wardrobe
and opened the door
and something brushed past
my shoulder,
it was invisible.
I went back and sat
on the edge of my bed.
It was only then that ghosts
entered my head.
I sat there for a while,
contemplating the fact
that the room was haunted
before I ventured back into
bed and fell asleep.

Once again, the knocking began
and this time I stayed in bed.

There was knocking
throughout the night.
I had very little sleep.
I arose from bed
with the arrival of a sunny dawn.

I realised that I was being haunted
and was completely lost
as to what I should do.
I soon got my head together,
over a cup of tea and with

a warm, beautiful, sunny morning.

That night I went to bed
in trepidation
but had no more
of the ghost's presence.
I was able to sleep soundly.
In the morning,
I awoke feeling as fresh as a daisy
and hoped that the haunting
of the previous night
was just a one-off
but that was not to be.

On the third night,
the spirit returned
and kept up the knocking
on the wardrobe.
I stuck it for about an hour
and then I was struck
with sheer bloody hatred
of the ghost.
I leapt from the bed
and charged over
to the wardrobe
and flung open the door,
punching into thin air,
air-fighting you might call it.
Eventually exhausted,
I climbed back into bed

and lay there,
heart pounding and sweat on my brow.

After a while,
I gained my composure
and the knocking had ceased.
For roughly thirty minutes,
I listened intently
but, thank Christ,
the room was silent
and I drifted off to sleep,
to rise in the morning
and listen to the songbirds
as I drank my morning tea.

Now we leap to
November 2020
and this spirit has
haunted my bedroom
for three years.
He mostly does his haunting
these nights
by knocking on solid surfaces.
At the start, he would move items around
and turn pictures on their sides
which were hung on the walls.
On another occasion,
I awoke in the morning
to find my wristwatch
missing from my wrist.

Later that day,
I found the watch
three metres from the bed,
on the floor.
I was most bemused by this
and puzzled as to how the hell
had he removed the watch
from my wrist without my waking up?

I have become blasé
to his presence,
indeed, I even talk to him.
He answers back by knocking.
I have seen him twice,
once when I was sleeping
on the sofa.
On opening my eyes,
I was astounded to see him
standing to my right,
leaning over the coffee table
looking at a collection of
small antiques placed thereon.
He was all in black:
black jacket, black trousers
and black hair,
a youth aged around twenty years.
The image disappeared after two seconds.
The second time I saw him
was when I was climbing the stairs,
to turn in for the night.

At the bend at the top of the stairs,
I happened to glimpse behind me
and there he was,
also climbing the stairs.

I have adjusted to living life with this spirit.
These days,
I sleep easily despite the fact
that he might be
indulging in some knocking.
Sometimes he goes AWOL
from the room for up to a week.
Christ knows where he goes
and what he does.

So, you see,
from being outraged
at my first encounters
with 'Fred', I am now
in a frame of mind
where I tolerate him.
I wonder what happened
to him in life?

You sceptics of the supernatural
must think again for,
quite simply,
ghosts do exist.

CANCER PATIENT
FIVE YEARS ON AND COUNTING...

It is now almost five years since
the diagnosis of cancer was bestowed to me.
I have baffled the medics, my family and friends
by defying cancer and living beyond expectations.
I know the cancer is still active
within me.
The various wounds on my face
are becoming larger with one huge hole
heading directly for my right eye.
If I become blind,
then that will be the end,
I couldn't face suffering the loss of my sight
which is why I have gathered
a large amount of medication
in preparation for ending it all.

To be honest, I don't much care
now for living.
All the old side-effects of radiotherapy
are still with me. That, combined
with this dreaded disease, has made me into
a very pale shadow of the man I used to be:
extreme fatigue, vicious facial pain,

no taste, no smell…etcetera.

In the past three years,
Guy's hospital made me
two prosthetic noses.
The first one was a total disaster.
It had to be glued
around the wound of
the missing nose. Not only that,
it was extra-large.
I looked like bleeding
Snochel Geronty and NOT ONLY THAT,
it kept falling off!
I had a few
embarrassing moments when
on the street, I had to walk around
with my hand holding
the nose in place.

The wonderful medics at Guy's
made another nose, this time with
slots for elastic to go around my head,
no more of that filthy glue, thank god.

This prosthetic nose
was made much smaller than
the first example and fits me
perfectly, with no problems at all.

I gave the doctor and his nurse

a large bottle of rum for him
and a fancy box of chocolates to his nurse.

The N.H.S. at its best
and never to be surpassed.
My grateful thanks to those wonderful people.

I offer this advice to
anyone who has been diagnosed
with this filthy disease,
not to partake of chemo or radiotherapy
and if there are any other options, take them.
Operations, for instance, any options
as opposed to chemo…it grinds you down
to a sobbing wreck who cannot do the simplest of things
like getting in and out of bed,
like a fifty-yard walk to the local shop and so on.

I wish the medics had initially
taken off my nose instead
of the six-week treatment of radiotherapy
which of course, failed at the end.
I realise that I would probably have died,
in any case but better that than
the side effects of radiation.

JAQUELINE MARIA MORAN (nee COX)

The photograph of her
that I stuck on an old clock
shows her smiling.
She is dressed in a 1970s white trouser suit,
a lovely girl
with jet black hair.

This picture of her
is just one amongst many
and in all,
she is smiling. But, you see,
she was not always smiling in life,
in fact
she was quite sober,
taking life seriously,
along with me, her husband.

Jackie was of Asian descent,
born in Bombay and had
an English grandfather,
a soldier in India
who gave his descendants
the Anglo-Saxon surname of 'Cox'.

I met her in 1969 and for me,
it was love at first sight. She was a beauty.
We dated regularly, married,
had three daughters
and stayed together for forty-one years.

I loved her dearly
but I knew only too well,
that she had no love for me.
In all our years together, she never, ever said
that she loved me or hugged me,
not once.

When I proposed marriage
she said,
matter of factly
and without a smile on her lips,
'Why not?'

I used to wonder why she married me
and surmised that, in her past,
before she arrived in England,
she had loved a man
with all her being and as life goes,
she had lost him.
For the last twelve years of her life,
she became an alcoholic,
drinking that filthy concoction
Vodka, a rotgut
of the mind

as well as the body.
In her drunken rages
she would physically attack me,
punching, clawing and biting,
all over my body.
I would seek sanctuary with one or t'other
of my three daughters.
Despite the horrors
of those twelve years,
of hell,
I stayed with her for the duration.
The utter misery,
of the mind-bending horror of
those twelve years of hell cannot be described.
She was a demon when drunk
and it was of no use to reason with her,
although I tried many times
but you know how it is
to try to placate and reason with a drunkard:
it just does not work.
Once, I found her at two in the morning,
flat out and snoring,
lost in a drunken stupor,
on the lawn of our garden on a very cold night.
I picked her up, praying that
she would not awake
or else I would be in for another beating.
Climbing the stairs,
I entered a spare bedroom and put her,
fully clothed in the bed and covered her

with an extra blanket.
I tip-toed into the main bedroom
and with a sigh, climbed into bed
thanking the gods
she had not woken up.
Life with this woman
had descended into a pit of
total black despair.

And so, it went on.
I shouldered the burden
of her behaviour,
knowing that in any event,
I would always be there for her;
she had to be cared for.
I could not leave her to her own devices for she was a
danger to herself.

She died in hospital on July 3rd 2010.

I have shed many tears in my life
but losing her,
has been the greatest emotional trial
of my existence.
In the month after her death,
I would talk to her in my dark bedroom,
willing her to appear before me and
PLEASE, PLEASE, PLEASE
talk to me, my love.
But of course, all was silent

with no apparition.
All I saw
was the streetlight outside with a dull light
peering through the closed curtains.

Eventually, the thrusting dagger of melancholia
finally stopped stabbing and I could, once more,
look at her in the many prints of her image in these photographs.
That is all I have of her and a lock of her hair.
I pray that
she is at peace now and for all eternity,
my lost girl,
my only love.

My mother died
on December 4th 1993.

In death, as in mysterious life
my father died on December 26th 1993.
Boxing day
Thus, following her
as ever he did in life
just 22 days later.

If, in fact,
there is an after-life,
then I hope they share it
and I pray to the gods
they are content at last,
as they lived only for each other
to the exclusion
of everyone else,
including me…
their son…

THE END

Other books by author

Treasure hunting on a shoestring – June 2006